Circling Back

The American Land and Life Series

EDITED BY WAYNE FRANKLIN

Circling Back

Chronicle of a Texas River Valley

BY JOE C. TRUETT

Foreword by Wayne Franklin

UNIVERSITY OF IOWA PRESS 〔ɥ〕 Iowa City

University of Iowa Press,
Iowa City 52242
Copyright © 1996 by the
University of Iowa Press
All rights reserved
Printed in the United States
of America
Design by Richard Hendel

Frontispiece:
Tupelo gum slough,
Angelina bottom, 1972

Library of Congress Cataloging-in-
Publication Data
Truett, Joe C. (Joe Clyde), 1941–
    Circling back: chronicle of a Texas
river valley / by Joe C. Truett; foreword
by Wayne Franklin.
        p.   cm.—(The American
land and life series)
    Includes bibliographical references
(p.   ).
    ISBN 0-87745-530-9 (cloth),
ISBN 0-87745-531-7 (pbk.).
    1. Truett, Joe C. (Joe Clyde), 1941–
—childhood and youth.   2. Angelina
River Valley (Tex.)—Biography.
3. Ecologists—United States—
Biography.   4. Natural history—
Texas—Angelina River Valley.
I. Title   II. Series.
CT275.T8758A3   1996
976.4'18063'092—DC20
[B]   95-45506
                                          CIP
01 00 99 98 97 96 C 5 4 3 2 1
01 00 99 98 97 96 P 5 4 3 2 1

For Sam, Jed, and Kathy

The next generation

Contents

Foreword *Wayne Franklin*

There was so much space. Joe C. Truett writes of the lost world of the Angelina valley in East Texas. He was born there in the early forties, of people themselves born there, and its life and his own intertwined the way place and being used to for most humans. It was not a matter of conscious identification — a kind of local patriotism — but rather a feeling of belonging, a sense of the land's contours and special places so ingrained in his experience that he could have followed them or found them in the dark. The place was mapped in his soul. It only looked like a landscape; in reality, that was his boyhood stretched out under the Texas sun.

No wonder Angelina haunted him long after he had left it. No wonder he had to come back.

What resulted is this portrait of a place in time, its layers opened by Truett's care and love and curiosity. His going back for the funeral of his grandfather Corbett Graham in 1967 may have started his long meditation on the world Corbett had known and he himself had glimpsed, a world that now seems ancient as Truett sketches its features. Corbett's life spanned a good deal of this century and embraced many of the enormous changes that have swept over Angelina and the rest of America. He began his farming there with horses, kept cows and hogs in the open woods, used mostly the energy he could find or make locally, had neither plumbing nor electricity back then, and planted open-pollinated field corn; but even that early he had adopted fertilizers, and soon he turned toward hybrid corn, eventually fenced his animals in compliance with the new stock laws, and in the 1940s climbed on board a two-cylinder "Poppin' Johnny" Deere tractor rather than his sorrel horses, Dan and Stepper, to work the fields or gather timber or travel about the land. His son-in-law, Truett's father, moved farther from the past. He left the land when crop prices kept falling and made his living instead as a carpenter. In time, the Truetts bought a one-acre lot overlooking the lake that the federal government made where the Angelina used to flow. It was at Plum Ridge, the site of Corbett and Fannie Graham's first farm. Some of that farm had been sunk under the waters of Sam Rayburn Reservoir, but from the Truett home only a short walk led to the ghostly old house site. Today's Angelinos, passing nearby on the golf carts they drive around the leisure community of Plum Ridge, could hardly be farther away from their parents or grandparents.

Truett's eye for such changes is acute. He catches them nimbly and pins them like butterflies to the smooth fabric of his prose. But though he loves the old ways, most of all he is an ironist for whom pure nostalgia has little value. He knows that Corbett's style of farming, inherited from his own ancestors, made the chemical fertilizers of our century necessary because the relentless cropping of land depleted its nutrients and nobody did much to replace them. He reveals Corbett's fascination with the machinery that remade or indeed obliterated his world and, in fact, at last caused his death when the Deere went over and crushed him. People in this world conspire with the forces that undo them, out of appetite or need or just curiosity. Truett describes how Corbett, who helped clear the woods of Angelina for the timber, instructed him in the art of felling a single tree exactly where you want, and Corbett's grace and skill are evident and heroic. Only brute power — no grace or skill — is evident in the giant machine that, by the end of the book, we see grip and rip and cut off trees like sticks. The contrast is clear, and the loss is too, but so is the implication of Corbett in the later chapters of the story. If the longleaf pines and the hardwoods native to the area have been replaced by the loblollies that to Truett simply do not fit into the landscape, cheapening it and expunging part of its local signature and making everywhere seem the same, it is not the gargantuan apparatus of today's lumber companies that must bear all the responsibility. Big changes come by little cuts, and the tool or weapon is in everybody's hands.

Truett's unflinching honesty will not let him blame the destruction of Angelina on the corporations or the government, though both have their share of guilt. He envisions an older, more worthy age, but he also knows that we have lost touch with it because we wanted to. He laments the loss but also understands it. What makes his prose so moving, in fact, is the combination of honesty and lamentation; this is a tragic story precisely because it did not have to happen as it did but in retrospect seems so inevitable.

If anything redeems the world of Angelina, it is that kind of maturity of thought. And it is memory. For memory is this landscape's fourth dimension. Truett has an extraordinary talent for sensing and excavating the lower layers of the place. He starts from and comes back to his own sense of things past and builds from that to create a complex tapestry of human stories filling up and filling out the landscape. He reaches back in imagination to the Hasinai who lived here when the Spaniards and French first arrived in East Texas in the sixteenth and seventeenth centuries — it was a Hasinai woman the Spaniards called "little Angel," in fact, after whom they named the Angelina River. Much of the early Spanish interest in the region derived in turn from rumors of French activities there, activities owing to La Salle's fatal confusion of the Texas coast with the Mississippi delta he was seeking. Back beyond "little Angel" or the other Hasinai or Spaniards like Father Massanet or Frenchmen like La Salle (who was murdered by disaffected followers near the banks of the Angelina in 1687), Truett finds the dim figures of the region's ancient hunters, whose projectile points Corbett taught him to find. Moving in the other direction, Truett finds the modern figures who sought out timber, explored for oil, laid utility lines, built the railroads and dams and other "improvements." He finds, too, the ties that link Angelina with others who never lived there or never even knew of it, people such as LBJ or Henry Ford. Johnson's political fortunes are emblematized in the reservoir named for his longtime political associate; Ford's revolution did much to alter the face of this and most other places on earth.

In these and other ways, the Angelina country emerges here as a re-markably populated landscape. And it is a landscape whose structure comes less from geology or even human history than from the knowl-edge that informs the eye gazing out across it. If we share Truett's dis-tress at the substance of so many changes, we welcome the vision that enables us to see them for what they are. And we welcome the mind — as spacious (and as modest) as Angelina itself—that probes their meaning and their origins. Truett's writing, like the best topographic prose, is about a given place, seen sharply and deeply; but it is also about the world at large, the landscape of human life. We are, all of us, heirs of Joe C. Truett's Angelina country.

Acknowledgments

A mere set of acknowledgments seems a small offering in return for the help others gave in the shaping of this book. But until my well comes in, it will have to do.

First, there is Judy, who typed and retyped and retyped again, with few complaints about my inability to get it right the fourth or fifth time. It all would have been impossible without her.

Several who still live in the Angelina country deserve special mention. My mother, Versie, supported me with encouragement and information and corrected me when my memory failed. To her excellent recall goes the credit for reconstructing events and circumstances in the lives of Corbett, Fannie, and others before my time. My father, Boose, and brother, Jack, told stories by action and words. By simply being themselves, they remembered how it was and showed how it still is among the rural men in that country. My sister-in-law, Darlene, is the finest example I know of a woman who knows about the old ways of making do.

Literary critics made a major difference. Mary Schlentz told me when the words and images were right and when they weren't. She knows that a good critic says no more than yes. Peter Lent read the entire first-draft manuscript and put me back on track where I had jumped it. Sam said yes and no in useful places, and Judy offered commentary almost daily.

Two individuals who work in East Texas's woods deserve special mention. Dan Lay set this effort in motion, though it eventually chose a path of its own. He provided information and instruction by way of written material, discussion, and critiques of draft material. Bob Little spent a day showing me the way modern logging operations work.

Several others helped, sometimes unknowingly. Virginia Marshall preserved the story of the Grahams' trip to Rising Star, as told by Sadie Graham Marshall, who made the trip. Francis Abernethy gave me information and encouragement. Paul Martin liked the mammoth story. Kathy Stapp loaned me books on Lyndon Johnson. Jed cheered me on and told me of his own manuscript, which I hope he someday finishes.

Circling Back

1 The Angelina Country

There's a land beyond the river . . .
Traditional hymn, "When They Ring the Golden Bells"

When I picked up the phone and my father answered from the other end, I knew something had gone wrong. Neither he nor my mother ever called long distance; it cost too much money.

"Granddaddy died," he said.

Looking out the window where I lived in Tucson, I saw green mesquite trees blur against the Santa Catalina Mountains. Thinking stopped. A whirlwind spiraled dust across the vacant lot next door.

"When will they bury him?" I remember asking, and then, "Yes, we'll come."

Early the next day my wife and son and I started on the long and by now familiar drive to eastern Texas. Soon the sun came up, stabbing through the truck's windshield. The tail end of springtime flowers lined the road.

Tucson fell behind. The sun climbed higher in the sky, and the blue-green GMC ate steadily at the miles. By the time the sun had settled to the desert rim behind us, you could feel a hint of thickening green, of moister country. After dark we strained to watch for careless hill country deer that jumped across the headlight beam like rabbits.

Daylight found us entering that land I still called home. In the morning mistiness, the woods pressed close against the road. If I kept my eyes ahead, the trees looked as they had always looked — dogwood, beech, sweetgum, oak. But a sideways glance betrayed them as the screens they were meant to be: behind them you could see the clear-cut lands, infested with young loblolly pine.

Driving down the final lanes between those veils of trickery always called to mind, for some perverse reason, the words of Robert Frost:

> Whose woods these are I think I know,
> His house is in the village, though. . . .

And then I'd invent other lines to keep myself awake:

> His woods have lost their mysteries.
> He makes his living selling trees.

The pickup kept on. The air felt sticky, whipping through the open window. We passed Dam B Reservoir, rolled across the Neches River bottomland beyond, and climbed the hill where widely spaced holly and magnolia trees someone had left in a roadside pasture to shade cattle in summer reminded me of the woods that used to be there. We slowed for the turnoff that would take us out to Peachtree.

It was hard to keep from thinking that Granddaddy would not be there.

The people at the funeral looked old. The prevalence of gray sprinkled on the heads of men and peeking from the shawls of women alerted me that my grandfather had lived a normal span, though I had thought that he was younger. Mr. Ocie McBride, his long-time friend, had come. He helped my father, my brother, two others, and me take the coffin to the hole that gaped beside the grave of "Nama" Fannie. Mr. Ocie's suit would have fit someone taller, and he had rolled the cuff bands of his trousers up to keep them off the grass.

Corbett. I heard the preacher say the name, and others whispered it in conversation. My grandfather had been Corbett to his older friends.

His real name was R. L., just initials, but I don't think many people called him that.

My mother had called him Daddy. My father usually spoke of "Mr. Graham," to show respect, and my brother, Jack, and I would not have thought to call him anything but Granddaddy.

After the funeral, we drove to my parents' home. I walked the hundred yards up the lane to Granddaddy's barn. The crib, made to hold corn, had been built with cracks between the logs to let in air, and the roof extended wide beyond the walls.

Beneath one wing, I found the hammer mill. Its belt lay slack, as if waiting for the life given by the power takeoff of the John Deere tractor. I remembered how the mill's teeth whacked and whirred as they gobbled up the ears of corn shoved in. The mix of shuck, grain, and cob would disgorge into the trough, and the cows would wrap their tongues around the pulp and stuff their mouths.

I thought back to the years before the passage of the stock law in our county. Then Granddaddy's cows had eaten mostly pinewoods grass instead of corn. They had roamed the hills and bottoms. He would call them from the highest ridge with his peculiar yodel, and they would come if they could hear, mooing all the way. And on a frosty morning in the fall you could hear his wild woods hogs where the hickories grew, cracking nuts between their teeth and rustling through the leaves.

This had been his and Nama's country, theirs and mine. Our kingdom then had stretched from where I stood beside the hammer mill to ten miles north, outlined by the sky, the sand, and the Angelina River.

Standing by the barn, I could see the oaks and hickories of our hammock close against the back fence of the pasture. The hardwoods, and the quick gray squirrels that traveled branch to branch within them, continued for a half mile past the fence. Beyond that lay the sunny sparseness of the longleaf piney woods, with their spring-fed baygall thickets, their waving bluestem grasses, and their fox squirrels loping tree to tree along the ground. Longleaf, so different from loblolly, leaving room for other plants, generous to animals, slow to grow but enduring. If you traveled onward through the pinewoods several miles, you would drop into the Angelina River bottom. There, water and fertility had conspired to grow the biggest oaks and acorns, the best

Where water and fertility conspired. The edge of a slough in the Angelina bottom in 1972.

diversity of animals, and the greatest possibilities. Down its length the river flowed.

What was it that had made this land so special? Its emptiness of people, I suppose. Its variety, which promised some new animal beyond each hill, a different fishing hole around the next bend in the river. A complexity that decorated it with mystery.

Growing up in this western corner of the South had seemed an ordinary thing until I went away. Then, from the vantage point of retrospect and other places, it grew in stature. It glimmered like a gem overlooked by treasure hunters. At dusk that day beside the barn, I made a promise to myself to somehow keep it all from being buried in the Jasper cemetery.

Demands of daily life have a way of dimming promises, and many years have passed since my grandparents died. The land they knew has greatly changed. Those who live there now could use some help, it often seems, from them and others of their time who lived so close upon it.

I, too, have changed. Now the days I spent with them seem only part of a longer story of the Angelina country. One that started long before my time or even theirs.

Finally, it has come together. Perhaps it does not flow the same as Corbett would have told it, but I have tried to keep the spirit there and to tell the truth as I have seen it. He and Fannie would have liked that, I believe.

2   Clovis

Nosing in through a blizzard over Denver at thirty thousand
feet I think what the earth covers at Lindenmeier there far away
to the north — those men we never found of ten millennia ago. . . .
*   It would take a glacier to reduce us to chalk dust but . . . at*
Lindenmeier the hunters had the grace to tiptoe away with the
last mammoth. We never found them, only their flints.
Loren Eiseley, *Flight 857*

When I was younger, the possibilities for adventure and romance seemed endless. Hoeing weeds and chopping wood offered temporary inconvenience only; once I got the proper motions down, I could yield to daydreams and still complete the tasks to Daddy's satisfaction. Legendary characters hovered just beyond the garden fence, and I was each of them in turn.

I sewed a breechclout from the cut off legs of old blue jeans and kept it hidden in a rock cleft in the pinewoods. On solitary jaunts I would strip down to my underwear — it seemed indecent to go farther — and put it on. A brown-skinned girl with raven hair always watched, approving. The wind would blow, and I would race from hill to hill through waving grass, which cut my legs and made me wonder how the Indians did without long pants.

As time went on, reality more and more held possibility at bay. My parents and teachers had less romantic things in mind for me to do. The girls at school had pale white skin and rarely ever watched unless I drove a car, talked a lot, or bought ice-cream cones.

Dreaming faded. Books by those who called themselves anthropologists and biologists replaced my favorite book, *Little Tejas*, about a Caddo Indian boy. Only with a rare surprise would I glimpse the wind-tossed hair of that dreamtime woman standing at the margin of the wilderness.

More time passed, and the passion for searching out scientific truth waned. It became easier to dream again. Finally, the line between the legend and the real has dimmed, perhaps because what people call reality seems at times more fictional than dreams. I can seat myself beside a lamp before sunrise and spend the morning in a different time and place. I can travel back ten thousand years and more with Loren Eiseley, scientist and poet, to the Lindenmeier country in what is now northern Colorado.

Below me, I could see the twilight resting on the river's pools and dancing in its riffles. In the farther distance, the river disappeared into a valley that wound its way across a vast and open country. I waited, sitting on my haunches by a rocky outcrop on the hillside.

The glow of sunset faded, and the moon came up. A breeze rustled in the grass. It grew into a wind, and soon the surface of the land about me rippled like a horse's skin in fly time.

Rearing over flats that flanked the river, cottonwood and willow trees with swollen buds rattled in the wind. Their shadows whipped at a group of huts. Flaps of skin closed the huts against the wind. In front of some of them, frames of willow branches swayed and sagged beneath the weight of hides and flesh.

Impatiently, I stood erect in the new moonlight and pulled the cape of skin about me. I kept my eyes upon the nearest hut. Suddenly its leather doorway lifted, and a human form came forth and moved into the open; an arm reached high and stripped a willow framework of its meat.

Was it she? The movements were so like a man's that I could not be sure.

The figure moved into a thicket. For many moments then, silence.

I stilled the nervous travel of my hand along the wooden shaft of my spear. Then the shape appeared again, climbing up the hill beyond the bushes. A pebble rolled.

Another sound came, closer. The wind swirled. An old-man smell nudged around the rock face, and the aged one called Spearmaker shuffled into view, leaning on a staff and burdened with a leather pack. Satisfied, I reached a hand out to him; we turned together and began to climb the hill.

When we topped the rise, the wind consumed us. I felt it whip my hair, billow out my cape, and slide itself inside the skins that hung below my waist. It felt warmer than the day before and tasted damp, the way it should, for it swept in from the south, the land that no one knew. It smelled like greening grass.

We moved beyond the hill toward a hollow place. Here, before the people made their camp in this valley, I had seen long-horned bison wallow in the time of hair-fall. Beside the mud-cracked ground, Antelope Woman waited, with the man-child riding on her back and hidden in a cape of fur.

Moon shadows hid her eyes. But the light was strong enough to show the outlines of her body, lean inside the windblown cape. She stood erect, her legs taut like the antelope's, signaling readiness to move. My eyes drifted down her rounded calves to where they disappeared into her fur-lined boots.

We moved into the wind. The prairie darkened as a bank of clouds passed beneath the moon. Ahead, a dire wolf howled; I passed my hand along the shafts of my two spears and led the way.

Morning found us in a swale, chewing strips of meat. Rain dripped from my cape. As I reached into the bag of meat Antelope had brought, I thought back to the time ten summers past when I first had noticed her.

She had seemed different right away. Digging prairie roots with other girls, she had simply stood when I appeared, not fleeing as the others had. Later on I had found that she was Spearmaker's daughter.

Hunters came to Spearmaker for his blades of stone. His people lashed them to the tips of slender shafts and with them hunted bison, horses, camels, and smaller animals. I knew Spearmaker still could make bigger points, the kind that his tribe once had used for larger beasts, the kind I needed.

In the years following my first encounter with Antelope, I had roamed the unknown lands toward the home of warmer winds. Sometimes I went with other men, one or two, sometimes alone. Often I returned to visit Spearmaker to replenish my supply of points, which, after my encounter with Antelope, seemed to get lost or broken more often than before. Then, a year ago Antelope Woman had borne a child, and we had made a plan. We would leave this place.

Now, standing in the morning rain, I scanned the landscape to the crests of the ridges that surrounded us. Scattered trees and clumps of bushes broke the sweep of grass. Thickets here and there cloaked the ground where slopes steepened or rocks thrust from the soil. Valley bottoms hid in grasses higher than our heads, and from these emerged trails of animals, leading up the slopes to higher ground. Picking up my spears, I slung my bag upon my shoulder, and Spearmaker and Antelope came to their feet.

Around midday, the sky lightened in the distance, and by nightfall the rain had stopped. Near a stream we found a heap of driftwood lodged against some cottonwoods and, by digging into it, reached the duff not soaked by rain. Antelope built a bed of leaves. The old man and I made a roof of logs and branches.

Underneath the makeshift roof we curled, body packed against body, for frost still settled on the grass at night. At first I could not rest because the child made noises as it suckled, and the odor of the woman swirled about me like a heady fog. Finally, the tiredness of two days and nights without rest pushed me into sleep.

By morning the sun had chased the clouds away. We left the driftwood bed and hurried onward. Herds of horses fled before us, camels lumbered off in smaller groups, and cloven hoofprints in the muddy ground showed the passageways of bison. Once a pack of dire wolves stood and stared, and, when we looked back from a hilltop, we saw them nose with lowered heads along our trail.

As the sun went down that day, I caught sight of vultures rising like a whirlwind. An odor smote the air, and we hurried forward. As we neared the circling birds, we saw wolves assembled near a camel's carcass.

That night we ate. The choice parts had been consumed by the wolves and vultures, but flesh remained beneath the hide, between the ribs, and on the neck; such parts are always eaten last by predators.

Spearmaker used his fire drill to coax a flame from puffy tinder he had stripped from the bark of a juniper tree, and Antelope cracked the leg bones of the camel with a rock, sucking at the marrow.

Later, I watched the woman as she sat before the fire. Flames danced against her face, and a tear trail glistened. Perhaps she thought of those she had left behind. Soon she curled herself upon a mat of grass and slept, holding close the child to keep him warm.

Several days we walked, always heading halfway between the rising sun and its place at noon. Smaller streams we waded; larger ones we crossed by loosing logs from driftwood heaps and making rafts. The sun climbed higher in the sky each day, drawing sprouts of green from the prairie soil, and Antelope dug deep into the earth to find the roots.

Then we came upon a bloated bison carcass in the eddy of a stream. Antelope waded out, pulled it to the bank, and plunged her knife blade into its belly. Gases whistled out, lending substance to the air. She skinned the carcass swiftly, cutting with a thin stone blade held between her thumb and first two fingers, and I dragged the butchered pieces up to higher ground. That night we feasted.

Three days we camped in this place, daily eating our fill and drying meat in strips. Antelope made new shoes from the neck skin of the bison, with the hair turned to the inside. She sewed the shoes with strands of backstrap sinew. By night we slept beneath the bison's hide.

On the third day, two hunters stopped. I expected something before we saw them, for a herd of horses grazing beyond the river had stood long against the sky with their ears alert. When the hunters reached the riverbank across from us, I saw with some relief that I had hunted with these very men two years ago; they were wanderers as I had been, hunting at the forward fringe of settlement.

They poled themselves across the stream on a driftwood log, landing in the eddy that had caught the bison. I made a sign to Antelope, and she gave them meat. They packed the meat in leather bags and soon continued on their way.

Two days later as the sun settled toward the rim of the world and we prepared to camp where a flint-rock hill abutted on a river bottom, I found the sign I sought. Antelope had built a fire, and her father, having climbed the hill to reach a rockslide glinting in the sun, sat pounding stones together. I had gone to reconnoiter, as one always should before camping.

A hunter trains himself to notice, at some level just below the conscious, things that signal "out of place." Something in the copse of stunted trees ahead seemed wrong to me, and I stopped to find it at the conscious level. I saw branches lying on the ground, fresh scars marking where they had joined the tree trunk. The leaves showed neither brown nor wither; they were thus no casualty of winter snow.

I sniffed the air. The odor came to me then, and no doubt had been waiting in my nose for some time, hoping to be noticed. Rank smell of urine and, when the wind shifted, of droppings.

I listened. At first I heard nothing except birds and a wolf's howl in the distance. Then I heard a low-pitched rumble carried faintly on the evening air.

I trembled. Mammoths, and not too far away. I went back to camp and spoke with Antelope, and she put out the fire.

The old man must have known already, by some subtle signal I could not decipher, for I found him chipping flint beside the fire. In one hand he held an oblong rock. Striking its sharpened edge with a horse-bone hammer in his other hand, he split off a long, thin flake. Shifting the flintstone deftly in his hand, he removed flake after flake from the underside. He flipped the stone, peeled flakes off the other side, and soon held a finely pointed blade longer than his hand. Two final blows took a sliver lengthwise off each side, so that a finger-sized depression gouged the center of the blade from base to halfway down its length. It was pure magic.

He opened up the pouch he carried at his waist. He lifted out a piece of leather and unfolded it, bringing into view a group of sharpened stones to match the one held in his hand. They glistened, and I noticed Antelope edging nearer, casting glances at the flints while pretending to be busy taking strips of dried meat from her pack.

Spearmaker slid his fingers down the central groove of a point and over its rippled surface to the tip. I and the other hunters of the frontier lands all knew the old man's points had special powers in the hunting of the mammoths. Perhaps this was the first time Antelope had seen her father make the massive blades, for mammoths had receded to the frontier before her time. She had grown up seeing mostly smaller points, made to kill the smaller animals that the people of her band had hunted.

I brought my spears to the old man. He felt the edges of the blades that tipped them. Tapping lightly with the piece of bone, he sharpened the flint points.

In my dreams that night, mountains moved and rumbled. Lightning flashes turned to gleaming tusks. Hairy beasts pursued me, and their trumpeting spilled into the sky, echoing and echoing, and my feet moved as if they were caught in quicksand.

Next day Spearmaker and I found the animals before the sun had dried the grass. Antelope had stayed in camp. From a bluff we counted four of them, feeding at the margin of the river's floodplain. Watching how they moved about, we soon saw that the biggest one, a female with a calf, was their leader. That told us the proper strategy.

We must try to kill the big female. She would be the most dangerous if we wounded others. Killing her would leave the others leaderless, confused, and they might stay around for days, giving us a chance at more. A confidence built from lessons of the past began to soothe my blood. The old man took one spear and I the other, and we left the bluff.

The wind can be the wildest trickster. Always watch it closely, for it can switch and give your scent away. Keep it always in your face.

The sun plays tricks as well. Keep it off your body if you can, especially when moving sideways in the view of animals. If you see the beasts facing you, stay immovable and in the shadows. Always stay below the ridgelines.

A good hunter moves with little noise. An accidental step can roll a rock or snap a twig. Leaves rustle, especially once the sun has dried the dew. When nearing animals, you must move only when they move so they will not hear you.

The wind kept steady, the sun rose higher, and the animals made a constant noise — cracking of brush, swishing of leaves, chewing. I slid closer.

At last the great beast towered just ahead, her tail toward me. Then she turned, just right, leaving me a clear path to her belly yet facing away so she could not see me. I poised, waiting. The moment came — she reached to get a branch, and the sound it made when she pulled it from the tree sent me as a bird from cover. She never heard my running feet.

There is a place in the belly just behind the ribs where the hide is thin — here you must keep your eye. Too far forward and your spear will lodge against the cartilage that anchors the lower ends of the ribs. Too far back and the coils of the intestine will catch the thrust, and the animal may live for weeks. If you focus your aim just right, angle the spear forward, and thrust with all your strength . . . And if the blade is magic . . .

Blood gushed over me, like a spurt of water from a hot spring. I barely dodged a tree trunk leg as the mammoth swung about as swiftly as a saber cat. Spearmaker gave a shout to get the animal's attention, and I burrowed like a rabbit through the brush. A scream of rage, remarkably high pitched for so large an animal, deadened every other noise.

The trumpeting subsided. The ground shook and branches cracked. Gradually the sounds grew fainter, and then silence fell. Spearmaker and I stood together and watched the boil of dust that trailed the mammoths across the plain toward the river.

There is a kind of spirit that always follows men, watching, waiting at the edge of their camps and their hunting parties for moments such as this. It is a female spirit. A supreme exertion by a man brings her closer, and a triumph pulls her inside where she dances with a mad delight. She finally comes to rest inside your head, and the ecstasy she brings cannot be described to one who has never found a victory full of blood and fury.

The dust still hung in the air when I felt her come inside. She made my chest swell and my head dizzy. Spearmaker watched me, knowing. Then he turned his back, reminding me that I must let her out before too long or she would make me sick.

We withdrew to camp. The death of a mammoth always takes a while, even when the blade is magic and the aim is true. We would look tomorrow.

The next day we found her dead in a little glade beside the river. Blood oozed from the swelling abdomen where the spear had entered. The old man slit the skin on each side of the hole and retrieved the broken foreshaft with its blade before he beckoned Antelope to come and touch the massive carcass, this creature more revered than all others, this totem of his younger days. Then we set to work.

There are those who specialize in hunting, and there are those who feast habitually on the leavings of the hunter. These latter kinds are as good at finding sign of a successful hunter as the hunter is at following his prey. The two kinds need each other. The hunter fills the stomachs of the followers, who in turn stoke the spirit of the hunter. Apart, they cannot sate their appetites; together, they survive.

We had barely peeled the skin from the topside of the fallen mammoth when the scouts of the followers arrived in the form of the men to whom we had given bison meat two days earlier. How they found us I do not know, but they have their ways. We talked. They desired to fetch their tiny band, camped two days to the west. Spearmaker and I agreed.

They scurried away like ants that have found a beetle carcass and, four days later, a gaunt assemblage of four men, five women, and a child stepped into the clearing. I saw a gladness in the eyes of Antelope as the women hesitantly approached. She stood very erect then, and with gestures becoming the woman of a hunter, began apportioning the flesh among the newcomers.

Around the fire that night, Spearmaker told about the kill. He talked of plans we had made to build a clan of people who would keep ahead of the hunting grounds of the bison people and live on mammoth flesh. He looked around, silently inquiring, and the men, eyes glazed with overeating, hummed a satisfied assent.

The fire died to coals, and the knot of stars people thousands of years later would call Orion the Hunter sank behind the trees. Antelope and I made our bed in a place separate from the others, underneath the mammoth skin which we had draped upon a framework of poles and brush. The spirit of the mammoth had built a fire within us both, and it was long before we slept.

The years passed. Our clan grew many hunters strong. Antelope gave birth to four more children, and three survived. In our camp there was always meat to eat and skins to wear. We drifted south and sometimes east, because the mammoths seemed to move that way. Bison-eaters from the north kept moving southward, too, pressing on our flanks.

Spearmaker grew feeble. One day he suddenly went searching for a special kind of stone. He retreated into solitude, chipping and flaking with his fading strength, and later he gave me the spearpoint he had made. The connection with the ancestors.

The next morning, he did not rise from his bed. The life had left him quietly, quickly, like a shaft in flight. Antelope and I stacked stones over him, and our band prepared to leave that place. I put Spear-maker's flint in a leather pouch I always kept at my waist.

We moved far then, to the south and east, entering a land where plants grew lush and streams flowed slow and brown. Leaves of many kinds lay underfoot in winter, and trunks of trees that dwarfed a man rose high above the ground. We set our huts on a flattened piece of land that overlooked the floodplain of a river.

The ancestors had told us how to pick a site for long-term camps. Look for a place adjacent to variety, they said. Diversity in animals, in plants, and in features of the land gives greater choices of animals to eat and plants to use. When some kinds of food get hard to find, walk the other way from camp and find a different kind.

In my foolish youth I had looked for mammoths only. It had worked, for a time. But now my aching bones bid me listen to the wisdom of the ancestors. We cleared a bigger space among the trees and built more huts.

Antelope grew to love this place, for there were foods of many kinds in addition to the meat of larger animals. She found fish, nuts, fruits, and roots of water plants. Shells from mussels the women gathered from the bottoms of the streams soon rose in heaps beside our huts. Over time we changed our dwellings, replacing drafty, temporary shelters with warmer, longer-lasting ones.

In this land we at first had found little sign of other men, but many beasts. Mammoths roamed the land, and mastodons, and many hoofed creatures. Nearly everywhere the trees stood far apart, and hunters could see game at many spearthrows' distance. Mastodons and mammoths pruned and crushed the smaller trees and brush and let the grasses in; they ripped the bark from larger trees when other food was scarce.

Streaks of light that fell to earth during storms started fires that swept across the land and lit the skies at night. New grass growing afterward drew mammoths and bison. Our people learned to fire the grass each year to bring the grazers within hunting range of camp. The people's numbers grew.

Year followed year. After some time I noticed that we were beginning to eat a lot of smaller animals. The great beasts had grown fewer; hunters everywhere said so. Soon the people numbered more than mammoths. Trees and bushes started creeping into openings and, despite our burning of the grass, I could not see as far ahead as when the larger beasts had kept the woodlands thinned.

One year in fall I found a curious mound of stone across the river from the village. It sat beside a swampy glade near where a creek spilled into the river's floodplain. A crack beneath a massive cap of rock gave shelter from the rain. I split some stones scattered there, and they showed impressions of the leaves of trees I had never seen. Afterward I went there often, for the place had a mystery about it. Perhaps it was the doorway to the Spirit Land.

Then came the year my grandsons, the hunters now, could find no mammoths in the country stretching from our village to the Endless Water that they said lay seven suns to the south. I began to think more of the Spirit Land where the ancestors lived. On occasion when I rubbed my arms, the limbs that once had plunged the stone-tipped shafts into the mammoths' hearts seemed as bones in bags of skin. My eyes, which once had read the mammoth trails and knew the vulture's language, clouded over so that I could scarcely see.

The snow-white geese with black-tipped wings announced the coming winter, as they always had. Seated on the lip of land that overlooked the floodplain, I could hear them flying southward, calling to each other. Antelope drew near. We talked about the hunts of other years, when we were young. I could barely see her hair, graying now, moving with the breeze. I reached for my pouch and Spearmaker's flint.

I felt the edges of the point, then the sides. I could see it clearly in my mind, a beautiful gray and brown. It had never killed a mammoth or even graced the tip of a spear; it lacked the fluted sides. I felt it slip away to the ground, but Antelope was there, finding it, pressing it into my hand. I could hear the mammoths trumpeting, drawing closer. Soon they would be here. Soon.

Three years before Corbett died, I left Texas to go to school in Arizona. There I circulated in the lofty air inhabited by professors at the university. The ideas they put forth sometimes rattled my previous notions of reality, and it took a fair amount of thinking to find out which ones made sense and which ones were ridiculous. Later on it came to me that the most important thing I learned there was not so much the ideas but the way to sort out sense from nonsense.

A notion that at the time seemed to me pure nonsense came from a young professor there named Paul Schultz Martin. Martin studied paleontology. He specialized in the plants and animals that had lived on earth during the Ice Age, or Pleistocene epoch.

Martin had a passion — the large mammals that had become extinct at the end of the Pleistocene. Most other paleontologists agreed with him that over forty kinds of this megafauna — ranging from mammoths and mastodons to animals related to modern-day camels, horses, and bison — had suddenly disappeared from the earth ten or eleven thousand years ago. But few agreed with him when he proposed a reason: Ice Age hunters sweeping into the New World from Asia had killed them off. I likewise snickered, secure in the infinite wisdom conferred by youth and a considerable experience hunting armadillos with homemade spears and bows.

The years passed beyond college, and the sometimes uncomfortable habit of picking up new information and reassessing old notions led to a disturbing possibility: there could be a grain of truth in Martin's "overkill" hypothesis, as it had come to be known. I had seen chunks of yellowed mammoth ivory excavated from Alaskan river gravels, carved and sold as trinkets in the fair at Anchorage. I had read in magazines and scholarly journals of new discoveries of flints found among long-buried bones of mammoths and other Pleistocene megafauna. Perhaps most disquieting, what I had learned of North American plants, of the dietary flexibilities of large plant-eating animals, and of similarities between parts of North America and the grasslands and savannas of Africa, told me something was amiss. American landscapes I had previously thought normal with their contingents of familiar grazing animals — deer, pronghorn antelope, elk — began to seem unnaturally vacant.

To learn more, I began in my spare time to trail the mammoth hunters. Some initial backtracking proved necessary. The spoor started at a place called Clovis, New Mexico, a thousand miles westward from the Angelina country.

One day in 1932, at Blackwater Draw near Clovis, two amateurs searching for prehistoric artifacts made an unusual find. Along what had been an ancient lakeshore they discovered projectile points made of stone. What they found seemed at first little more than commonplace, but the discovery caught the attention of scientists for two reasons. First, the points were constructed differently from arrow-heads ordinarily found at ancient Indian camps. In general they were larger and more finely worked, and they contained a lengthwise groove, or flute, from base to midpoint or beyond on both sides, presumably a slot to better hold the split end of a shaft. Second, bones of mammals long extinct lay among the points.

Years later, after further digging, archaeologists pronounced that some of the bones had come from Ice Age mammals. Some thought that human hunters might have speared the mammals with the points that lay among their bones. They named this type of spearpoint "Clovis," after the nearby town.

The story of the Clovis points gained momentum after new techniques had been applied at other archaeological digs. In 1949 Willard Libby at the University of Chicago discovered a method to tell how long ago plants and animals unearthed by archaeologists had lived. He found that, by analyzing the atomic structure of the element carbon in pieces of wood, charcoal, or sometimes bone, he could estimate their age.

By the 1980s scientists had assembled radiocarbon dates of many sites in North America where Clovis points had been unearthed. A pattern appeared — all the Clovis points that could be aged had been left by people roughly eleven thousand years ago. It seemed that people did not use these points after mammoths and mastodons had become extinct. These clues led some to suspect that early humans in North America had fashioned Clovis points specifically to hunt mammoths and mastodons. Cautiously, supporters of Martin's ideas eased new papers into print. But one should not be too bold; one might lose respect or, worse, tenure at the university.

Evidence from present-day hunting tribes indicates how and why humans might have exterminated big animals. Explorers and anthropologists in Africa have found Pygmies armed with spears killing elephants. Big animals have more value than small ones to people who hunt to make their living; this leads to greater hunting pressures on the larger beasts. The Ice Age mammals in the New World may have been particularly vulnerable to human hunters, which they had never before encountered. Large mammals reproduce slowly; more rapidly producing smaller animals such as deer and bison could have subsidized bands of people while hunters killed the last mammoth, the last mastodon, the last ground sloth.

꘎Thirty years after I first heard Paul Martin give voice to that unthinkable hypothesis, his car rolled into my front yard in western New Mexico. Mary Kay, his wife and traveling companion, came from behind the wheel of the maroon Mercury Cougar. Martin exited the other side. Once more I had cut the trail of the mammoth hunter, but this time with more knowledge of the tracks he followed.

In anticipation of this meeting, I read a story he had written called "The Last Entire Earth." A scientific summary of Pleistocene extinctions, it commented on the emptiness of present-day North American landscapes. The last entire earth disappeared ten thousand years ago with the mastodons and mammoths, Martin said. More than a century earlier, Henry Thoreau had written of his desire to experience the "entire earth" that had existed in New England prior to the settlers' extermination of many of its large animals.

Martin's story contains a mystic quality that transcends science, a flavor that seems to have slipped from some ancient human gene pool past the filters of modern objectivity. "In the shadows along the trail," he says, "I keep an eye out for the ghosts, the beasts of the ice age. . . . Such musings add magic to a walk and may help liberate us from tunnel vision, the hubris of the present, the misleading notion that nature is self-evident."

Now, sitting in my living room, Martin recalled the 1960s when he had stirred up such a storm of controversy.

"I thought back then," he said, "that people soon would see the evidence and agree with me. Now, though some have come around to my way of thinking, it looks like convincing the majority will take more years than I have left."

We talked about the human tendency to cling to time-worn explanations of reality and to reject the new. We talked of Africa, parts of which he once had toured in a small airplane and from which he had returned more convinced than ever that his ideas were justified. We talked about the future of bigger animals worldwide.

"The pity is," he said, "that most conservationists can't see the North American continent's potential for preserving in the wild many of the large mammals that soon will face extinction in Africa and elsewhere. We've been educated with the dictum that alien is bad. The irony is that most of us are aliens ourselves."

The fire still burned. Finally, he stood, tall and gaunt, perhaps in another life the wielder of a Clovis spear.

"Give us some advice about where we could drive to see elk," he asked.

"Back roads are no problem," said Mary Kay as I looked apprehensively at their vehicle. "This car has seen a lot of off-highway travel."

Then they were off, to make a circuit of the high country. To look for elk, bunched tightly and watching from a meadow or scattered out among the firs and pines, alone now where once they had grazed along with bigger beasts. Perhaps the Martins would pull the car up to some lip of land and stop to listen for the sound of heavy-footed animals moving just beyond the edge of vision. To feel the ground for the tremble caused by fleeing herds of those other occupants of the last entire earth.

3　Corn

And the Lord God called unto Adam, and said unto him,
*　　where art thou? . . .*
. . . Hast thou eaten of the tree, whereof I commanded thee
*　　that thou shouldest not eat? . . .*
Therefore the Lord God sent him from the garden of Eden,
*　　to till the ground. . . .*

Genesis 3 : 9, 11, 23

"I'll bet you can't find one with an odd number of rows," Corbett said as we sat pulling the green shucks off the "rostnears" of corn.

I checked the rows of kernels on each pearly white ear we dropped into the tub. By now I could count by twos. Sixteen. Fourteen. Eighteen. Sixteen.

Nama Fannie seemed to know it was no use counting. She cut the corn two rows at a time. Holding an ear in her left hand, palm up, she used her right hand to pull a butcher knife with its cutting edge toward her from the far end of the ear to the near end. The moving knife sliced off the tips of the grains, while somehow always missing her thumb and fingers. Following each stroke, she shifted the ear slightly to bring the next two rows upward. I watched. The rows always came out even; there was never an odd row left to cut.

After she had cut the grain tips off, she scraped the ear, again two rows at a time. Angling the knife blade almost perpendicular to the ear, she pushed it away from her, and the juicy cream flowed out the severed heads of the kernels and into the pan held in her lap. She scraped once around the cob, then reversed it and finished the job with another round of scraping. Near the end she wiped her knife against the cob every few strokes to clean off the last bits of corn.

My mother silked the corn prior to the cutting and scraping operation. This required removing with a smaller knife the hairlike strands I later learned carried the pollen from the exposed patch of silk at the head of each ear down the cob to the kernels. On some ears, kernels clamped the silks very tightly between their rows of grains, and I could never clean them out as thoroughly as she could. The silks I left showed up later as brown threads in servings at the table.

"You boys better get another load of corn," Corbett said as we neared the bottom of the shucking tub.

My brother, Jack, and I took the number three metal washtub by the handles and trundled into the acre-sized garden behind the house. Corn took up half the space. We walked between the rows, fending away the leaves to keep the sharp edges off our faces. We looked for ears with the bottom half of the exposed silk pale and soft and the upper half brown and dried, peeling back the shuck now and then to see the kernels and check our assessment of the ear's readiness for harvest.

Corbett had showed us how to pull the ears. Grip with your left hand the stalk at the bottom of the ear, then grab the top of the ear with your right hand and yank outward and downward. Pop! Squeak of shuck. Thump into the tub. Smell of newly picked corn.

Corn worms lived in nearly every ear. They cut mealy trails among the kernels near the tip and lodged just below the thatch of partly dried silk. Green ones, brown ones, fat ones, and thin. I contested with Jack to find the biggest. We saved them to toss into the chicken yard and watch the rooster race to them and call the pullets with a cozy "putt-putt," which we translated roughly to mean, "Want some candy, girls?"

One tub heaped with stripped cobs and another overflowing with shucks signaled a trip to the barnyard fence where the cows waited, drool stringing from their mouths. Before letting the cows eat the cobs, we had to chop the cobs into two-inch sections with the "hack knife," a stubby machete fashioned from a piece of a broken crosscut saw. If you failed to cut the chunks of cob short enough, one might lodge in

Corn-shucking team. Corbett, Fannie, and their grandsons in the mid-1940s.

the gullet of a greedy cow, and that required reaching your hand past a raspy tongue and down a slimy throat to pull it out.

That night we ate corn, cooked for an hour and stirred frequently to keep it from sticking to the bottom of the pot. That old field corn, the grown-ups later called it to distinguish it from the sweet corn that eventually took its place at our table. Thick and pasty when cooled, it bore little resemblance in taste or texture to the sugary soup I poured years afterward from store-bought cans labeled "creamed corn."

Corn always overshadowed other crops as the manna of the farmstead. Corbett's pair of sorrel horses, Dan and Stepper, rumbled the dried ears around in the bottoms of their troughs and crunched the grains off the cobs with their front teeth. Corbett carried stunted ears of corn he called "nubbins" in his saddlebag to feed to hogs that roamed the nearby woods, to keep them halfway tame. The hog dogs fed on loaves of bread Nama baked from ground-up corn — kernels, cob, shuck, and all. We ate cornbread ground from our own corn at the local grist mill; sometimes it was the hot-water kind fried in fritter form, and sometimes it was pie-shaped loaves baked in thin pools of hog lard.

In the earliest days I remember, Corbett and Fannie lived with Corbett's father, "Pa" Graham, at his old homeplace that edged against the longleaf pine woods. Corbett grew corn in the sandy soil of the back hill pasture, and they stored it in the pine-log crib. My brother and I played about the corncrib, climbing on the piles of corn, sliding to the bottom, and always keeping watch for a wood rat that old Grayboy the cat might have missed.

Pa Graham in his old age was a very private man. He seldom spoke as he rocked on the front porch gallery in his rawhide-bottomed chair. He maintained his outdoor toilet in a red oak grove a hundred yards beyond the split-longleaf pickets that enclosed the front yard of the house. He scorned to use the nearer backyard outhouse. My brother and I discovered his structure, an icon of simplicity, and soon got into trouble with Pa.

What attracted our attention was not the main structure — a horizontal pole two feet off the ground wired to a tree at each end — but the store of cleaning implements. Inside a rusted five-gallon can wired on its side to one of the support trees, we found a stash of corncobs. Some cobs were red and some white, and all had that new-shelled fuzz, with the appropriate shape for post-relief cleaning. Soon we were pushing the tips of sharpened switches into their soft cores and flinging them at each other in a furious corncob battle.

When Pa finished his toilet the next morning and reached for a cob, the can was empty. We learned of his rage from our parents, who scolded us severely. We drooped away with properly downcast eyes, but I glanced back and saw them smiling secretly at each other.

Both my grandfather and my father cultivated corn according to tradition. Instructions had been handed down from their fathers and their grandfathers before that and modified by that magical product of twentieth-century technology, commercial fertilizer. Lay out shallow furrows three or four feet apart and dribble the gray, lumpy dust from the 5-10-5 fertilizer sack down the trenches by hand. Bring out seeds saved from last year's crop, drop the grains by hand a couple of feet apart in the furrows, and cover them with the plow hooked to Old Dan. When the corn sprouts, keep a gun handy for crows, or they will walk the rows, pulling up the new green seedlings one by one.

In my early school days, Corbett grew corn in a six-acre field surrounded by hardwood hammock land. The field lay on a hill a quarter mile through the woods from home. What struck me even as a youngster was the difference between its pale, crusty soil and the dark, leafy loam that wrapped around your feet like a sponge in the nearby woods. I believed back then that Corbett had purposely selected this place to put the cornfield because of the difference in the soil; only later did I learn that the farming itself had gradually hardened the soil, removing its nutrients and organic matter and putting it in annual need of the 5-10-5 potion.

I also later learned that sandy and loamy soils in a warm, high-rainfall country have scarce supplies of nutrients. Once cleared of trees, the soil loses nutrients to crops consumed by animals and people and to rainwater leaching downward into lower layers beyond the reach of crop roots. By contrast, the original forests had recycled in place what nutrients were near the surface and with long, searching roots had brought others up from the depths.

Corbett had no tradition of recycling soil nutrients. Rather than spreading cow, horse, or human manure on fields, his forebears had responded to fertility depletion by moving on — from Alabama to Mississippi to Texas — and carving new openings in old forests. By the time the frontier ended, commercial fertilizers had come along to revitalize depleted fields.

The fertilizer makers brought together potash and phosphorus from mines in distant places and nitrogen manufactured from the natural gas produced in oilfields. These they mixed and put in bags labeled with the percentages of each in the mixtures — 5-10-5 and many other options. They shipped the sacks of fertilizer to farmers, most of whom had little notion of the great amounts of energy that had gone into the mining, processing, and transporting of the nutrients.

There came the time when hybrid corn replaced field corn. Increase your bushels per acre, said the *Farmer-Stockman* magazine. Early in the spring, Corbett brought the seeds from town, and that fall we opened the shucks to ears of a uniform golden yellow. But we still could find none with odd numbers of rows, and furthermore, each year now you had to buy new seeds at the feedstore.

Corbett probably never had heard the term "Green Revolution" and most certainly would not have knowingly participated in any war against convention. But by adopting commercial fertilizer and hybrid corn, he became an unwitting soldier in the campaign toward mechanized crop production that began as a formal revolution in the 1940s. Application of commercially produced fertilizers and pesticides coupled with new plant varieties bred to thrive under such conditions boosted crop production dramatically. The downside was that all the ingredients had to be bought from distant producers, and thus the farmers lost a tiny piece of independence. But that slipped from notice when everyone joined the revolution.

By the 1950s, even with hybrid seeds and the cheapness of the new fertilizers, most small-scale farmers could not make a respectable income from the sale of crops alone. They needed more cash than previously — store-bought goods considered luxuries only a generation earlier had become social necessities. Furthermore, leaps in crop production nationwide had driven market prices down, and large farmers held a competitive edge over small ones.

"You can't make a living farming anymore," I heard my father say one fall when I was very young. This happened shortly after he had sweated for a summer plowing twenty acres of corn with a horse and shortly before he went into the cabinetmaking business.

After I left the Angelina country for graduate school in Arizona, I ate corn that had taken a more complicated route from soil to table. I bought cornmeal from the El Rancho grocery store in Tucson, which perhaps had received it from a packinghouse in Chicago, which may have gotten it from a nearby mill, which had bought it from a Midwest cornfield. It was just a sack of dry meal. It had lost the flavor that had been built by bare toes digging into springtime soil and northers rustling corn leaves in the fall.

The Arizona land was full of rocks. It got little rain, and the only crops I saw growing there were irrigated from a pump or ditch. The towns were filled with people far removed from the land. But the Arizona countryside, though different from that of my younger days, had its own hidden stories to tell. By learning its plants and animals and getting out into it, I began to hear the stories and feel more and more at home. Finally, one day I stumbled onto a familiar track and began to wonder if the mystics were right after all, that life is a circular journey and that you eventually come around to where you started.

The track turned up on a high plateau. In that stony land I had grown accustomed to wearing heavy boots, even in summer. On that particular day, I had hiked far into a sandstone canyon pockmarked with crevices and holes. I came across a curious wall of masonry someone had built in the shadow of an overhang. I clambered up and over the wall and found more stoneworks, among them a semicircular bin plastered against the rear of the shallow shelter.

Once my eyes became accustomed to the dimmer light, I looked into the little bin. On the surface of the soil inside lay several objects that resembled short cigars. I picked one up, put it into better light, and sat back in astonishment. The cigar had taken on the twin-rowed checkerboarding of a cob from a tiny ear of corn. I unlaced my boots, peeled off my socks, and rested. The skin on my feet looked shriveled and sun starved. I rubbed my toes into the dusty soil on the shelter floor.

Then outside I heard a rustling, as if in a breezy cornfield. But when I looked, the sun showed only a broken agave stalk scratching itself against bone-dry leaves.

Beyond lay the silent, silt-floored canyon, dotted with a scattering of sage and grass. I listened.

Suddenly I imagined I heard a distant shouting. For a moment, just a moment, it echoed from the cliffs, sounding like the calls of children playing, perhaps chasing one another in and out among ancient stalks of nubbin corn. Then the babble stopped, and there were only swifts, twittering and diving in the emptiness.

I began to find small corncobs in other places, sheltered from the elements. Cobs turned up in cliff-wall clefts reachable only by makeshift ladders or by shallow handholds artisans had chiseled in the rock. They appeared where ancient wanderings of streams had carved recesses into bluffs. They lay in museum trays where archaeologists had placed and labeled them.

Books that told how many years the little cobs had lain inside the crypts astounded me. A thousand years perhaps, and in some cases maybe twice that long. Cobs that would disintegrate within a year under Angelina's rain and sun had survived for centuries in the dusty caves of Arizona and New Mexico. The growers of the corn had vanished three hundred years and more before Columbus came, killed or sent away by some mystery that has yet to be deciphered.

Archaeologists and anthropologists tell us that humans as intelligent as modern people lived on earth for hundreds of thousands of years before they learned to farm. Planting crops for harvest started only ten thousand years ago or so, in the Middle East and Asia. Before that, people fed themselves solely by hunting animals and gathering plants from forest and savanna.

When people started farming, they set the human species on a different course. Very soon, in terms of time since people's beginning, farming opened access to unprecedented plenty. Roving bands of people settled down in villages, which grew and became towns, then cities. The wealth of food that farmers grew fed others, some of whom devoted energies to art and architecture. Farmers sowed the seeds of civilization.

In the unfarmed landscape, most of the sun's energy goes into plants that people can't easily use for food or clothing. Farmers change all this. They sow their fields with plants that best convert the sun's energy into products needed by people; others they eliminate.

The sun shining on the Angelina forest built trees, which fed squirrels with their fruits and nuts. A beech tree provided a squirrel or two per year for a person to eat, if the person could catch the squirrel. A corn patch, using the same amount of space and sun energy, provided many times that quantity of human food.

The more efficiently the farmer funneled sunshine into making human food, the more the human population grew. This always has been so. History instructs us that, as farming people begat yet more people, the more they built about themselves the trappings of civilization: cities, social classes, and, of necessity, more fields for growing crops.

Archaeologists say that farming in the New World started seven or eight thousand years ago. The plants that would become the staples — corn, beans, squash — did not instantly appear but took shape gradually. People made them into more and more efficient food producers over several thousand years of selection and experimentation. Corn, in Columbus's time the major food of North American Indians, had originated in the highlands of Mexico, probably from a wild plant botanists call teosinthe.

Transfer of crop seeds and farming technology from region to region seems to have been very slow during the early years. Corn, grown for food in central Mexico at least five to seven thousand years ago, appeared in what is now the southwestern United States only about three thousand years ago. Perhaps another thousand years elapsed before it made its way to the American Southeast, by which time squash and some other plants were already being cultivated there.

Archaeologists believe that, in both the Southwest and Southeast, the importance of corn as food may have increased rather gradually over many human generations after it first appeared. During this time, people must have selected for better corn varieties and more efficient farming practices. Eventually, corn became the major food and led to much larger populations than before. Some scientists now estimate that, at the time of Columbus, the North American Indian population exceeded ten million.

Once people had made the full transition from hunters and gatherers to farmers, they could not go back. They numbered far too many to live on gleanings from the wilderness. They who had partaken of the knowledge of tilling the ground were henceforth compelled, as God had decreed upon expelling Adam and Eve from Eden, to eat bread by the sweat of their faces.

Glenwood, in western New Mexico, lies in the morning shadow of the Mogollon Mountains. The San Francisco River slides down from the north, roaring past Glenwood when in flood, but more often than not whispering. When it leaves the little valley, it runs westward through a gorge into Arizona. Geronimo, the Apache warrior, raided here in the early 1880s, and shortly thereafter Butch Cassidy found the little valley a fine hideout between train robberies. I moved there in 1991.

The San Francisco valley lies in the center of the region called the Mogollon Highlands. Archaeologists say this region claims a special place in the annals of human occupation of the present-day United States — corn grew here first. Eventually it spread to other regions of the country.

East of Glenwood, U.S. Forest Service Trail Number 214 leads into the Mogollon Mountains. First it climbs onto a mesa. Then, about three miles from town and just before the trail reaches the foot of the mountains, a dim, unnamed path angles off to the bottom of a canyon where there is always water. If you look sharply about you on the lip of land where this spur drops away, you will find a curious stone arrangement — straight lines of rocks take the form of an eight-foot square barely protruding from the earth. Pieces of broken pottery lie here and there, and once I found an arrowhead.

Archaeologists call similar structures pithouses. These dwellings were used by aboriginal Americans in the Southwest two to three thousand years ago. By late in the pithouse period, these people had grown corn for a thousand years or so, and larger villages had taken shape near the major streams.

I am certain that the stone square beside Trail 214 once was a pithouse, which over the centuries lost its roof and filled in with soil. Remnants of thousands of pithouses lie among the Mogollon Mountains; I find them on level terraces near streams where junipers give way to pines and cottonwoods. These places are quiet now.

Between the homeplace of these corn-growing peoples and the Angelina country lies a vast, semiarid flatland where bison ranged and hunting tribes always prevailed. From college years onward I often drove Interstate Highway 10 or its predecessors across this reach, ticking off the thousand miles and feeling changing states of mind as the vegetation changed from west to east — desert grassland, dune mesquite, Texas hill country juniper and live oak, blackland prairie, poorland post-oak, and finally, pine and hammock land.

I would hate to walk it, but perhaps someone did, for corn showed up in the Angelina country and eastward about the time of Christ. Ironically, the first East Texas corn could have come from the very Mogollon Mountain valley in which I eventually settled. I like to pretend that it did.

❧I suppose weevils and rats got the last of the field corn Corbett used to grow. Today I do not know if any like it exists — seeds from those kinds of plants are now called heirloom seeds. An organization in Tucson that collects old varieties sent me some corn called Texas Shoepeg, and from these seeds in Glenwood I grew short and very thick ears with kernels like pegs. They sent blue corn also, from a tribe in the Sierra Madre of northern Mexico, and some Navajo corn with small, white ears. These all thrived when fertilized with manure, and I now save seeds year after year.

In late spring when the sun rises warm over the mountains, it is time to bring out the corn seeds, pull off my boots, and wiggle my toes in the soil. This land has become familiar to me now, and it smells like sustenance. Perhaps this will be the year when I grow an ear of corn with an odd number of rows.

"A boy's will is the wind's will,
And the thoughts of youth are long, long thoughts."
Henry W. Longfellow, "My Lost Youth"

June 1958 marked the beginning of my second high school vacation. Early one morning I fought the drowsy comfort of sleep and pulled myself from bed before daylight. By the first gray light I had eaten breakfast, called the feist dog, Squeeze, and left a dark trail in the dew across the pasture.

Where a thin road plunged into the woods, I turned to look back. Our house stood white against the trees across the pasture; Corbett's house hid in water oaks a couple hundred yards beyond. My fifteenth year was on the wane.

As I turned and started down the long-abandoned roadway, cherry laurel trees and yaupons leaned into the opening, flinging spiderwebs across the gap. I broke a branch to sweep the webs away before they wrapped around my face. Excitement gave each step a spring; today I knew that I would find the fabled Hole-in-the-Rock.

The roadbed took me north, following an old-field stand of young loblolly pines to the right and a brush-and-briars tangle of a twice-cut hammock to the left. An armadillo halted in the lane ahead, lifting up its nose; it had heard my step. Squeeze gave chase, and the armadillo raced into the hardwood tangle, disappearing in a hole beneath an old magnolia.

Fifteen minutes later I could feel the woods begin to open up. The ruts had whitened now with sand. A fox squirrel flitted up the red oak that marked for me the entrance to the piney woods, and Squeeze stood by the tree, looking back at me. Ten minutes more and I would come upon the fallen cones of the first longleaf pine, where on windy days the sound changed from a rustling to a soughing.

"Follow Hog Creek down across the Tennessee Gas pipeline," Corbett had repeated just the day before. "Before you reach the Angelina bottom, the flats beside the creek will start to widen out. On your right you'll eventually come across a little glade, and on the other side of that, if you look sharp, you'll see it, rising up and looking out of place.

"What's that? No, there ain't nothing else like it anywheres up there. You'll know it when you see it."

By the time I crossed the arrow-straight woods road we called the Old Kirby Main Line, the sun had lighted up the longleaf tops. The washed-out road that led up the hill from there to Pa Graham's place had cut through sand and down into a bricklike soil, where rain had gouged a ditch and chunks of gravel perched on stools of red-brown clay.

I lingered briefly at the old homeplace, vacant now that Pa Graham had died and Corbett and Fannie had moved nearer to us. The huge red oaks overhung the sandy yard as always, but the cypress shingle roof sagged where a gallery post had fallen through the rotting porch. The straight-up boards of longleaf pine still stood beside the dogtrot that ran between the two main parts of the house, but the white mud chimney had started to disintegrate. I removed the cistern cover to sound a "ho" and hear an instant "ho" bounce back from the bottom.

This last vestige of human settlement for several miles marked the commencement of the real piney woods. Sand sucked at my feet where the road traversed swales. I could see a hundred yards and more in most directions. Longleaf trees towered over scrubby sandjack and

Here we lounged, cooling off. Corbett's "wash hole" on Hog Creek in a remote stretch of longleaf pinewoods.

blackjack oaks on the flats and ridges; baygall thickets hid the watercourses trickling from the hillsides down to larger creeks. I loved these woods.

About two miles down the road I ran into one of those situations that in minutes shoves you into a new age bracket. It happened just before the road ruts climbed a hill to cross the pipeline corridor.

I had passed a baygall head on the left when Squeeze began to bark where the open woods merged into a thicket of wax myrtle. When he came into view, he was moving my way and looking back over his shoulder with his tail down. I knew he hadn't barked at an opossum or squirrel.

Then I heard that awful sound of a riled-up hog bent on mischief.

It wasn't a grunt or squeal but sounded more like a raucous throat-clearing repeated over and over.

Several months before, three big hogs had come coughing out of a beech grove at me nearer home when Squeeze had barked at them. That time I had yelled at them and fired my Winchester .22 rifle into the ground in front of them before deciding they were not about to stop. Then, looking back over my shoulder and remembering the size of tusks on hogs we'd butchered, I had set out at a near-panic walk and left them behind.

This time I wasn't going to run. No sir, these hogs could come right up if they wanted to, but I'd bluff them out. I shifted the rifle to my left hand and looked around for a stick. Near at hand lay a hefty pine knot, the club-shaped heartwood of a limb from a rotted longleaf. I could use the .22 as a backup.

When the hogs came into view, I relaxed a little. There were several, but I couldn't see any really big ones, males that might have two-inch tusks. I remembered Corbett's stories of hogs disemboweling dogs and slashing legs of horses that he rode. One time I had seen him sew back a slab of meat nearly as big as my hand where a tusk had ripped it from the hog-dog Belle's hip.

Squeeze moved behind me, barking, and I knew that wasn't good. Hogs can't see you very far if you don't move, but they zeroed in on the noise and kept coming. I yelled as they came, but that only made the larger ones raise the pitch of their rattling. They shouldered against each other, finally stopping in a menacing semicircle several feet away.

They had moved past the distance where flight seemed an option, so I simply stood with club shouldered. It felt comfortable, like a baseball bat does once you've learned to hit well. Corbett would probably wave his arms and give a "heah!" and they'd run away, I was thinking, when the biggest one charged.

I knew woods hogs could move fast, and that old sow did. She dashed forward, turned her head sideways, and opened her mouth, reaching for my leg. I could not later remember launching the pitch-filled club, but then you only remember the baseball flying over the left-fielder's glove and not the swing. The sow gave a piercing squeal, falling back against her audience. They scattered.

Well! I hitched up my pants, raised the club to knock another pine knot off the fallen log, and moved on. Squeeze ranged out as before, looking for squirrels. I knew that today I would find Hole-in-the-Rock.

Shortly I crossed the right-of-way that marked the course of three buried metal pipes, occasionally exposed where they bridged steep ravines. Through these pipes the Tennessee Gas Transmission Company pumped natural gas from South Texas petroleum fields to power plants and fertilizer factories farther east and north. We called the grassy strip across the land simply the pipeline, and it served as a convenient landmark. I never thought of it as the corridor for transport that it was, a symbol of human ingenuity in distributing energy and raw materials across the country.

This day, as usual on my trips toward Hog Creek, I turned off the road and moved northeastward on the pipeline right-of-way to climb a hill. To the northwest through the tops of scattered longleaf pines that cloaked the hill, I saw the land fall off toward the Angelina River, still two miles away. Northeastward, beyond the hill, a low place marked where the south branch of Hog Creek crossed beneath the pipes on its way to the river.

About a quarter mile up Hog Creek from the pipeline crossing was the favorite swimming hole of my brother and me. Below a six-foot waterfall, a hole had worn into the soft-rock substrate, and below that, another hole. Here we lounged at midday, cooling off from the long walk in. Corbett had shown it to us years before. He had called it the old wash hole, which no doubt described its function in his youth.

I dropped to the creek, looking for hog or deer tracks everywhere a bare ditch slashed across the hillside. To see a deer in those days occasioned telling and retelling. Constant hunting, never mind the legal season, kept them scarce and wild. Hogs far outnumbered deer, for the carvings in their ears made it risky for a man to shoot one not his own. Respecting local marks of ownership while ignoring game laws made in town showed the common precedence of custom over new-made law.

Many a deer hunter kept a pack of hounds — Walker, bluetick, black-and-tan — to chase the deer across a woods road or the pipeline where another hunter with a load of buckshot sat. On a day like this in early summer, you might find a dog box on a trailer waiting to collect the dogs that had chased a deer so far they couldn't hear the master's horn. One such trailer often parked down from this hill at a crossroads that we had named Houndville.

So far I had not seen a vehicle, or a person, and the two seemed usually inseparable in these woods. But I had not expected to run across anyone, except maybe a deer hunter, for those who ventured far from settled places seemed compelled to justify it by some practical purpose — to hunt or fish, to look after hogs, to cut wood for fence posts. Most kids my age stayed in town.

Turning left at Hog Creek, I soon began to scan the reaches of its bottom. At first the pine hills squeezed the little floodplain tightly, so I hurried on. Within the hour the bottomland commenced to widen, and to search it thoroughly I had to crisscross the flat on the right-hand side. Nothing came to view but trees and shrubs festooned with brown needles of longleaf pine. The Angelina bottom must be just ahead, I thought. It began to seem like once again I'd missed the place.

Clouds had covered up the sun. Now I heard a distant rumble, reminding me of one main reason for my search — shelters from the weather were uncommon in these woods. Several times I'd been soaked, once petrified by lightning, and often kept at home by pending rain. A refuge in the center of this vacant countryside would help.

Giving up a systematic search, I pushed ahead, thinking that another hour would put me near the old abandoned Warner farm where Hog Creek met the river. The rickety two-room house with its newspapered walls still kept out the rain.

Then I stopped. Across a grassy glade a mound took shape. It blended, ghostlike, with the background, for shrubs and trees grew on it and fallen leaves had covered it. I walked closer. It seemed the most unnatural thing I'd seen among these gentle slopes and flats.

Blackness marked a hole that opened near the bottom. Stillness held the darkening woods, as it often does before a rain. Slowly I drew near, breathing easily but feeling my heart race.

The hole grew larger as I moved closer and gained a different view. The sides seemed smooth at the entrance, as if the rock had split apart at some time in the geologic past. I saw the bottom of the little cave, flat and leaf covered, running back into the dark. A tremendous slab of rock, angled slightly, capped the whole affair.

Sanctuary in the Angelina woods. Looking out from Hole-in-the-Rock, Hog Creek, in 1960.

Some kind of critter might live in there, it seemed, and maybe rattlesnakes. Shelters such as this were hard to find. I eased closer, put a hand upon a rock near the opening, and slowly leaned to peer inside.

Suddenly a thumping issued from the hollow. I clutched the .22 more tightly. I tossed a pebble at the sound. Silence. A minute passed.

Venturing another step, I leaned farther over. A pale and fuzzy ball took shape in a patch of daylight far back in the tunnel. It moved; it thumped. It hissed! It turned into one of two baby vultures, white as snow.

Raindrops pattered on the fallen leaves, then quickened to a downpour. I rested with my back against a rock inside the entrance to the cave. There comes no better time than rain when you have a shelter snug enough to keep the water out but small enough to let the sounds and odors in. I pictured Mother Vulture waiting out the rain some-where on a leafless snag above an armadillo carcass.

Had other people used this cave? If so, they left no evidence, no writing on the walls. Corbett knew about it, even had a name for it. The trees that rimmed its hidden glade stood in silence.

When the rain stopped, I climbed atop the mound of stone and peered into the other crevices that reached into its innards. Pieces of loose rock felt soft but brittle, and I hit a small flat piece against a mas-sive boulder. Curiously, it split itself down the middle. Opening its lichen-covered flatness like a book, I beheld a sharp and perfect image of a leaf.

A strange and unfamiliar leaf it was. Corbett had taught me local plants; I knew them all, and this did not belong with them. What geo-logic age and habitat had spawned the fossil leaf, I could not know.

Trees bent in a sudden wind. Clouds scudded faster overhead. I stuffed my pockets with more rocks and called for Squeeze. It was after dark when we got home, and the folks had worried.

5   Trade Winds

Whither, O splendid ship, thy white sails crowding,
Leaning across the bosom of the urgent West,
That fearest nor sea rising, nor sky clouding
Whither away, fair rover, and what thy quest?
Robert Bridges, "A Passer-By"

My first venture into trade and commerce came in the early grades through an obsession with marbles. Nearly all the boys and a few of the girls dealt in marbles. The school yard served as the trading rendezvous. Here we brought our goods and made our transactions.

The currency of trade, loosely called marbles but encompassing several kinds of small spherical objects, had value mostly because of the status conferred on the possessor, though with marbles you also could buy candy bars, pocketknives, and other things of functional value. Opaque, standard-sized marbles constituted the basic and lowest units of currency, the one dollar bills. Similar-sized but scarcer were the "cat-eyes," clear glass marbles with irregular wisps of color in the interior; until they became common, they traded for several ordinary marbles. Glass "log-rollers" approaching an inch in diameter brought more, perhaps ten or fifteen plain marbles. The ultimate in scarcity and desirability were the "steelies," shiny ball bearings of various sizes that had come from the dismantled wheels of trailers, cars, and Caterpillars.

Trading marbles locally when you lived in a rural area brought little excitement, for few traders lived within walking range, and they invariably owned marbles that only duplicated what you already had. Traders from a wider range of lifeways could be found on the school grounds; they might bring rare and exciting options from an upper-class variety store or an auto body shop. Cousins in distant cities offered the most thrilling opportunities, for sometimes they had marbles and marblelike items never seen before at school.

Games of skill and risk involving marbles gained more popularity than straight trading, and every spring during most school recesses boys gathered around rings in the sand encircling clusters of marbles. Each player had contributed to the cluster. Contestants took turns shooting at the clusters, each shooter propelling with his thumb a marble from the margin of the ring and claiming all marbles he knocked out of the ring. Rather plain-looking marbles might thus gain value as a well-known "shootin' taw." I once traded a white and badly pitted taw for a handful of regular marbles and a steelie.

A few boys persisted in ignoring the gaming regulations in force and made up their own self-serving rules. These individuals usually displayed a general disinclination for regimentation and self-discipline — they typically shot marbles poorly and made bad grades in school. Some resorted to covert thievery. Most disconcerting, a loosely organized band of them invented an activity called "scrapes," in which a person lingering at the outskirts of a marble game would suddenly swoop through the ring, scoop up the marbles, and race away. Yelling "scrapes" loudly as he did so legitimized his thievery, at least among the bandits.

≋People who hunt and gather things from the wild to sustain themselves have found, like the marble traders, that to get the best mix of resources they must move around. A common feature of nonfarming tribes is their mobility. They shift from place to place with the seasons, following the availability of animals and the ripening of plants. Some range widely and may spend different years in different places. Surely they always have found, as any modern hunter knows, that nature's bounty never distributes itself uniformly.

Domesticating plants and animals did not completely solve the problem of uneven distribution of resources. Farmers, who by necessity placed permanent homes beside moist and fertile soils, often had to range into the hinterlands for scarce commodities. Thus farming villages sprang up where mountains met the flatland, where forest merged to prairie, or where streams cut through the hills. Cities formed where rivers yearly dropped their fertile silt on fields abutting uplands that provided building stone and grazing lands.

Trading came about as a way of giving people access to a broader range of things. The secret to the trader's wealth lay in bringing locally uncommon goods from other places. Many a priest and king built their power base by moving goods from place to place.

The most successful traders used the best transportation available. In my grade school days, everyone rode free to the trading rendezvous on buses, with their marbles in their pockets. Those who had families that traveled regularly to Jasper, Beaumont, or even Houston claimed an advantage, unfair we rural boys thought, because they gained free transportation to the marble kingdoms of faraway places.

Early on in human history, captains of commerce found that they could extend their trading forays to economic advantage if they traveled on water. A traveler could float a greater load downstream than he could carry over land. So men built rafts, then clumsy boats. These gave way in later years to sleek canoes.

People floating on the water felt the spirit of the wind. When it blew upon their backs it made the journey shorter. They lifted up an animal skin and then a canvas sail. To catch the wind, to ride on water, brought the goods of distant places closer to the towns.

For many centuries now, people have been making epic voyages by water. At least forty thousand years ago, travelers ventured out of sight of land to cross from Southeast Asia to New Guinea and Australia. Four thousand years before the birth of Christ, Polynesians crossed vast stretches of ocean to settle on far-flung Pacific islands. A thousand years ago, Viking ships sailed from northern Europe to Greenland, Labrador, and Newfoundland.

Circumstance surrounding early civilizations catalyzed some leaders to build trading empires based on wind and water. Since before the time of Christ, nations on the Mediterranean Sea built bigger civilizations by trading on the power of the wind. Then, half a millennium ago, southern European traders near the ocean made a quantum leap: they broke the bonds of coastal waters and sailed away to make their fortunes on the "dark side of the world."

In the fifteenth century, the technology of sailing began to build upon itself, and ships spurted farther seaward. The Portuguese, then the Spanish, French, and English, moved offshore using the stars to guide them. Information stored on paper kept the ships on course. Scholars developed astronomical tables and charts of ocean waters. Records of the paths of sun and stars led to improved navigating instruments.

Priests, kings, and merchants seeking wealth doled out motivations. Prince Henry the Navigator of Portugal, both a scholar of sailing and head of the Order of Christ, sent explorers along the coast of Africa in the middle of the fifteenth century seeking slaves and gold. The Portuguese soon rounded southern Africa, looking for a route for trade in spices of the East.

Christopher Columbus sailed from Spain, looking also for a trade route to India and the East, but he landed in America instead. This accident foretold unprecedented change for the Angelina country.

Columbus reached the islands that we know as the West Indies in 1492. Other Europeans had found the New World long before this, but the technology of sailing and the demand for resources had not then been great enough to provide an impetus for colonization. This time was different; soon a permanent settlement sprang up in the West Indies.

A quarter century after Columbus's expedition, Hernando Cortés discovered an unbelievable store of gold in the Valley of Mexico and descended on the Aztecs there in a classic "scrapes" maneuver. Within the next twenty years, three other Spanish explorers — Pánfilo de Narváez, Hernando de Soto, and Francisco Vásquez de Coronado — entered what is now the southern United States in search of steelies. Finding only common marbles, they pulled out in disgust, leaving behind trade trinkets, religious messages, and germs from European diseases. A lateral movement from De Soto's expedition came very close to the Angelina country.

After these early Spaniards left, quiet settled over the forests of the Angelina country, even more intense than before de Soto's men came through. Straw houses fell vacant as the Indians fell from disease.

Survivors probably gathered at the better sites to plant their corn and hunt deer and turkeys as before. Only those Indians who journeyed far to the south and west beyond the river that the Spaniards called Río Grande del Norte reported seeing the bearded men in crusty clothes.

A century and a half passed before Europeans re-entered the Angelina country. This time they came to stay. Their advance messenger bore the name René-Robert Cavelier, Sieur de la Salle.

La Salle came into the world with economic advantages. His mother occupied high steps on the social ladder in the seaport town of Rouen, France. His father and uncle had made fortunes in the sea-bound trade.

In 1666, at age twenty-three, La Salle set sail for Canada, landing at the French stronghold at Montreal. He quickly learned the languages of local Indians. One day he heard some visiting Indians tell about a river to the west that drained a region rich with buffalo and furs and which flowed into a southern sea. His imagination bled upon his ruffled shirt; he conjured up images of empire, ruled by the French from a fort that he would build at the exit of this waterway into the sea.

In April 1682 La Salle, with other Frenchmen and some Indians from New England, traveled down the Mississippi River to its mouth. In the manner of the day, he claimed for France the entire drainage of the river, ignoring any claims of native tribes that inhabited the region. He named the territory Louisiana, in honor of his king. Then he retraced his journey, ascending the Mississippi, the Illinois, and back into Canada.

Two years later he returned to France. He asked the king to give support for the fortress he envisioned on the lower Mississippi. He described the wilderness of furs the river drained, common marbles but nonetheless abundant. The king consulted with his minister and gave La Salle four ships. Agents of the king rounded up recruits, and the company that set sail in July 1684 included soldiers, gentlemen of wealth, families, unmarried women, missionaries, and many "volunteers" snatched from seedy parts of town.

Disaster beset the expedition from the start. By the time the French reached Santo Domingo in the West Indies, their main provisions had fallen prey to Spanish buccaneers. La Salle sandwiched fits of sickness between violent arguments with the captain of the ship that carried most of the remaining stores. Worst of all, the final landfall found them on the Texas coast far west of their expected destination, the mouth of the Mississippi.

Joutel, a trusted soldier from Rouen, after having floundered about on shore with a crew of men, summed up the situation: "The trouble was our great number of men, and the few of them who were fit for anything except eating. As I said before, they had all been caught by force or surprise, so that our company was like Noah's ark, which contained animals of all sorts."

Finally La Salle decided they should disembark where a series of lagoons skirted the coast. He proclaimed water moving between passes to be an outlet of the Mississippi. They would settle here. Many of the passengers moved from ship to shore.

Soon a band of Indians attacked those on shore. Shortly thereafter, the remaining supply ship wrecked in the shallows. Three weeks later, Beaujeu, a captain often at odds with La Salle, took a crew of men and left for France in another of the ships. La Salle, his brother, his nephew, Father Anastasius Douay, Joutel, and the other colonists retained only a small frigate, which soon also wrecked.

They were clearly stuck. The wind that had sped them there from France could not be caught to take them back.

La Salle fanned his dreams with desperation. Under his instruction, a rude structure made partly from the wrecked boats commenced to rise on the low and marshy land beside the sea. Preferring to emphasize its glorious purpose rather than its modest proportions, he christened it Fort St. Louis. The Indians watched it take shape on the banks of what is now the Lavaca River, just before its entry into Matagorda Bay, Texas.

Misfortune grew. A foray from the fort convinced La Salle that the Mississippi lay some distance eastward. Indians continued to harass the colonists. Some men plotted a rebellion but were thwarted. Two men deserted, and another died of snakebite.

Spring passed, and more men died of disease contracted by debauchery during their sojourn in the ports of the West Indies. The remaining colonists, never models of discipline, became even more useless. People survived on crops from European seeds hastily sown, on buffalo they shot nearby, and on fish caught from river and lagoon.

The last day of October 1685 La Salle with fifty men set out northeastward to find the Mississippi. He left Joutel in charge of the men and women at the fort. After weeks of travel, the expedition found a large river, which they mistakenly took for the Mississippi. They built a fort beside the river and left several men in charge of it. La Salle and the remainder of his force turned back, reaching Fort St. Louis in rags near the end of March 1686. La Salle fell sick again.

When he recovered, he outfitted twenty men, including Father Douay, from the dwindling stores at the fort and set off once more on the same route he had followed the previous winter. He intended to ascend the Mississippi and Illinois Rivers to French settlements in Canada. Once again, he left Joutel in charge of Fort St. Louis.

Beginning the trip on April 22, 1686, they trekked over prairie alive with buffalo. They reached and rafted the Colorado River. At some point they apparently decided that the Mississippi lay beyond the terminus of their previous journey.

They passed through woodlands and hacked their way through canebrakes to the banks of either the Trinity River or the Neches, it is difficult to tell which one in retrospect. Here the numerous "Cenis" Indians (Hasinai, a subgroup of the Caddo) took them into their grass huts. The French found the insides of the houses to be adorned with Spanish trinkets — silver lamps and spoons, swords, musket parts, and money — brought by Indians traveling trade routes north from Mexico.

Moving eastward from this place, La Salle soon fell ill again, as did his nephew. The procession stopped for two months for the invalids to recover. For the first time, Europeans had penetrated the heartland of the Caddo Indians for a lengthy sojourn. Not since the brief passage by de Soto's men nearly a century and a half before had white men seen the woodlands of the Angelina.

While La Salle mended in the shade of the Hasinai summer, Father Douay reflected upon the Indians. Despite the probable effects of epidemics introduced generations earlier by de Soto's men, Douay found the Hasinai "numerous." The elixir of corn had done its work. Douay wrote in his diary:

> This village, that of the Hasinai, is one of the largest and most populous that I have seen in America. It is at least twenty leagues [about 60 miles] long, not that it is evenly inhabited, but in hamlets

In the woodlands of the Hasinai. Spanish "moss" brooded over the Angelina
country when the Spaniards made their first entry.

of ten or twelve cabins, forming cantons [subdivisions], each with a
different name. The cabins are fine, forty or fifty feet high, of the
shape of beehives. Trees are planted in the ground and united above
by the branches, which are covered with grass. The beds are ranged
around the cabin, three or four feet from the ground; the fire is in

the middle. Each cabin holds two families [Joutel later said eight or ten families per dwelling].

Douay became distressed at La Salle's long illness and recorded their actions:

> ... our powder began to run out; we had not advanced more than a hundred and fifty leagues in a straight line, and some of our people had deserted. In so distressing a crisis the Sieur de la Salle resolved to retrace his steps to Fort St. Louis; all agreed and we Straightway resumed our route, during which nothing happened worth note but that, as we passed the Maligne [Brazos] River, one of our men was carried off with his raft by a crocodile of prodigious length and bulk.

La Salle's party reached Fort St. Louis this time laden with corn, beans, pumpkin seeds, and melons they had obtained from the Hasinai. But even these did little to lift the veil of despair that had settled upon the colonists. Of about two hundred left behind when Beaujeu had sailed away, fewer than forty-five remained. The graveyard held more bodies than did the fort itself.

A more determined attempt to reach Canada seemed in order. After a brief rest, La Salle organized a new expedition, this time including Joutel. Twenty stayed behind; over half of these were women and children.

Once again the travelers passed northeastward over the prairie, meeting Indians almost daily. They sheltered themselves from the rain under fresh skins of buffalo that they killed along the way. They used buffalo hides for shoe casings and made a buffalo-skin boat with which to cross rivers.

Quarrels broke out anew. A man named Duhaut, together with the expedition's surgeon, Liotot, conspired to kill La Salle. The plot reached its consummation deep in Hasinai country, near present-day Wells in the split of land that separates the Neches and Angelina Rivers.

On the night of March 17, 1687, Duhaut and Liotot camped with three of La Salle's followers some distance from the place where La Salle camped. Liotot approached the sleeping trio, axe in hand, and with surgical precision split their heads. Three days later, when La

Salle came looking for his friends, Duhaut and Liotot ambushed him. He fell with a bullet through his brain. The pair then stripped the corpse of clothing, leaving it for scavengers.

Duhaut took control. Joutel, Father Douay, and the others went along, unwilling prisoners. Duhaut and Liotot hatched a plan to travel to the Mississippi, where they would build a vessel and escape to the West Indies. Joutel called this "a visionary scheme, for our carpenters were all dead . . . besides, we had no tools for it."

Without the technicians and the technology, the power of the wind could not be captured. Duhaut and Liotot seemed oblivious to their dependence on the tools of industry and the skills of specialists.

Joutel found among the Hasinai three Frenchmen gone native, deserters from La Salle's visit the year before. Tattooed like Indians, they seemed to him only at close range to be "civilized men." One of these deserters, a Breton sailor named Ruter and a previous associate of La Salle, soon joined forces with a buccaneer named Hiens and slew the murderers. La Salle stood avenged. The Indians stood amazed at the violence of the white man.

Joutel, Father Douay, La Salle's uncle and nephew, and three other survivors set out for the Mississippi and French Canada. They found the river this time and, after an arduous journey upstream, reached Montreal. From there they sailed to France. They told their story to the French king, who decided to pretend that the fort erected in his name on the Texas coast had never existed. He left the remaining colonists there to their fate.

Sieur de La Salle, harbinger of change, had been killed, as often befalls messengers, but the seeds had been planted. Other Europeans soon would come to vie for possession of the Angelina's resources. They, like La Salle, were interested more in drawing lines around ordinary marbles than in making a rapid getaway with steelies. Furs, deerskins, human souls, and real estate would soon gain prominence as currency.

6 A Beast in Hand

Little Bo-peep has lost her sheep,
And cannot tell where to find them;
Leave them alone, and they'll come home,
Wagging their tails behind them.

Nursery rhyme, "Little Bo-peep"

Ghosts of long-dead tribes inhabited the woodlands of my younger years. Arrowheads and sometimes pieces of broken pottery marked old campsites. I envisioned the daily lives of Indians as having been far less regimented and thus a great deal more exciting than mine. Part of my planning for an eventual escape from schoolwork and mundane chores to that earlier and more nearly perfect state of being entailed a lot of practice on weekends and during school vacations.

Expeditions into the woods of only a day's duration sufficed to remind me of the greatest need — food. How to meet this need without having to work a garden started to simmer more or less continuously in the background of decimals and long division.

I began to launch "survival" trips. Getting food, even after I graduated from a slingshot to a .22 rifle, proved harder than I had envisioned. Breasts of cardinals and thrashers spitted over a fire provided pitifully small servings, much less than my stomach demanded. Even squirrels were not always easy to kill, and in cold weather armadillos kept to their burrows. Grasshoppers, though tasting better than I'd imagined, seldom sufficed for more than hors d'oeuvres. The grown-ups held their tongues, probably with some effort, but Corbett did show me how to call a bobwhite quail and make a bird trap out of split pickets.

After exhausting the grade school library, buying the *Straight Arrow Injunuities* woodcraft manual from the shredded wheat cereal company for fifteen cents, and talking with Mama, Daddy, Corbett, and Fannie about things their parents and grandparents had eaten, I began to think about plants as food. I gathered pokeweed leaves — poke-salad, they called it — from new-cleared ground in springtime. It tasted like spinach. I sought hickory nuts in fall, soon becoming discouraged with the time it took to pick out the flesh. Oak trees, especially white oak and cow oak, yielded a lot of acorns in some years, but I couldn't figure how to get rid of the bitter taste. It all seemed a scant harvest and very unpredictable.

I became curious about how the animals managed. Ground tracked and scuffed by woods hogs centered in fall on acorns, hickory nuts, and beechnuts; in spring the hogs grazed new weeds and grass and un-earthed pine roots and, I guessed, all sorts of worms and insects. The blunt muzzle of the milk cow took in grass, weeds, and, when other food grew scarce, yaupon leaves. Our neighbors turned loose some goats in a fenced patch of brushy woods, and soon nothing green remained within five feet of the ground.

Grass, leaves, weeds, and roots went into experimental brews. Hardly any of the grass and leaves would soften up enough to eat, even when cooked for hours. The weeds and roots generally tasted very bad. A few things turned out satisfactorily — the fiery roots of jack-in-the-pulpit, for example, tasted okay when boiled for an hour and also worked wonders in the school lunchroom when I slipped an un-cooked slice into Jimmy Mashaw's mashed potatoes.

Later, in college, I found out why cows and horses could eat grass and I couldn't. Their stomachs contain bacteria that digest woody fiber, said the animal science professor. Grass and most leaves contain a lot of fiber called cellulose, and only animals with lots of cellulose-eating bacteria in their stomachs can get much nourishment from them. Human stomachs don't have these kinds of bacteria.

Furthermore, he said, the bigger the grazer, the tougher the forage it can handle. The food sits longer in a big animal's stomach, giving the bacteria more time to work. A cow can digest tough forage a lot better than a deer — those goats I saw that ate everything in sight might have been half-starved. Elephants eat stems the size of your finger.

I thought about that. I had seen Corbett's hog dogs eat grass, but then I had later seen the grass intact in their droppings. My curiosity about my own ability to digest grass never drove me to carry the experiment quite that far, so I just took the professor's word for it.

Though I never quite gave up on the idea of reverting to the wild, for the time it turned out to be a lot easier milking our Jersey cow and eating her calf. A lot of people had already learned about this, I later found out. They had been discovering and rediscovering it for several thousand years.

Domesticating animals to use as intermediaries between wild plants and human stomachs first took root about the time people started farming. Many anthropologists believe women initiated the practice, perhaps taming young animals as an extension of the female caregiving urge. In Europe and Asia people eventually made domesticates of horses, cattle, sheep, goats, dogs, and chickens.

Among these animals, dogs alone came with people on those earliest migrations from Asia to North America. After humans had established themselves in the New World, South American Indians tamed native llamas and alpacas, and some North American tribes began keeping turkeys. Curiously, a kind of chicken that produces green eggs and that we now call Aricana also turned up among South American Indians. No one knows quite how it reached there from Asia, where chickens originated, though some believe it might have arrived on boats with vagrant Polynesian peoples who colonized the South Pacific islands.

European colonists brought their beasts along with them on their explorations. None among the new arrivals so strongly helped the Spanish gain a foothold in the New World as did cows and horses. Columbus on his second voyage brought both to stock the island of

Santo Domingo. Within a few decades, these had multiplied, and colonists took some to the mainland. Ships from Spain hauled in more. Soon the lands about the villages in Mexico echoed with the animal sounds of home.

Cows and horses capture energy from grass and funnel it to use by people. Herders do not need to tend the grass on which the cows and horses feed, and the forage can grow on soils too arid or infertile to raise crops. Thus the beasts provide a source of energy that would be impossible for humans to get without the animals.

This energy can be packaged as a piece of meat to eat or a beast to carry burdens. The first permanent European colonists, the Spaniards, preferred eating cow, but some native tribes came to prefer horse. Both cows and horses served to transport goods and people over land. Spaniards and most natives seeking transportation preferred horses.

Both Spaniards and Indians in the Hasinai country found a beast in hand to be worth several in the bush. First, domestic animals required less energy to catch and use for food, and their young were less often lost to predators than were the young of wild animals. Second, except for bison, the native animals — deer, turkeys, bears — could not digest coarse grass and other tough forage, nor could the wild animals be put into harness.

The Angelina country, like other open woodlands in the South, seemed to be a paradise of grass waiting for a bigger beast. The biggest creatures — mammoths, mastodons, and others of the Pleistocene — had long since gone. The white-tailed deer and turkeys made little dent on the supply of grass.

Horses came into the Angelina country in advance of Spanish settlers. La Salle and his men found them there in 1685 — Indian horses packed the food La Salle brought back to Fort St. Louis on their first trip to the Hasinai. The Hasinai had obtained these horses from other Indians, who in turn had bought or stolen them from Spaniards at northern outposts in Mexico.

Soon after La Salle and Fort St. Louis perished, cattle came. They were herded up from Mexico by Spanish expeditions sent to hold the Texas borderlands against the French. The advance guard mowed wide strips in the Texas grass as they plodded up from Mexico in the waning years of the seventeenth century.

Excitement flew about the streets of Monclova, Mexico, on the first of Easter Feast, March 28, 1690. Sleepers in this northern Spanish outpost in Coahuila woke to hear a multitude of mules bray and horses whinny. Two hundred cattle milled about, bawling.

People looked out the portals of sun-baked adobe houses to see laden animals leave the town and move into the brush beyond. Quickly the supply train for Alonso de León's second Texas expedition to Matagorda Bay dwindled to a speck beneath a dusty pillar in the sky. Next day many soldiers followed.

Two horsemen with this caravan held high responsibilities. Alonso de León had orders from the king of Spain himself, filtered through the viceroy of Mexico, to set up frontier stations and thereby keep the French out of lands claimed by Spain. Father Damian Massanet looked for heathen souls to save among the Indians.

The French had catalyzed this expedition. Shortly after La Salle with his three ships had sailed into the Gulf of Mexico, word had spread. Like angry bees, Spanish sailors had boiled from northern ports in Mexico. They sailed along the northern Gulf, looking for La Salle's party.

In 1687 two Spanish brigs from Vera Cruz saw remnants of La Salle's wrecked vessels in the shallows at Matagorda Bay. Assuming that a colony had been established by the survivors, the Spaniards launched a series of expeditions overland from Mexico to find the French. De León, a soldier of Nuevo León and son of a pioneer of the hinterlands of northern Mexico, led the expeditions.

In the spring of 1690 de León moved his men and animals across the Río Grande and onward to the northeast. He and Massanet had ridden this part of the route before, almost exactly one year earlier. At that time they had sought and found the site of Fort St. Louis established by La Salle. Father Massanet had written an account:

> We arrived [at Fort St. Louis] at about eleven in the forenoon [of April 22, 1689], and found six houses, not very large, built with poles plastered with mud, and roofed over with buffalo hides, another larger house where pigs were fattened, and a wooden fort made from the hulk of a wrecked vessel. . . . There was a great lot of shattered weapons, broken by the Indians. . . . We found two un-

buried bodies, which I interred, setting up a cross over the grave. There were many torn-up books and many dead pigs. . . . The Frenchmen had a piece of land fenced in with stakes, where they sowed just a little corn, and had an asparagus bed. . . .

Not a living soul had been found. De León had seen three bodies, of which he said: "One of these, from the dress that still clung to the bones, appeared to be that of a woman. . . ." De León and Massanet had later learned, from deserters of La Salle's colony whom they found living with the Indians, that smallpox had weakened the colony near the end. Indians had killed most of the survivors, sparing two children and two others at the request of Indian women, who "carried them off on their backs."

Now in 1690, as March fled into April, the soldier and the priest retraced their tracks to Matagorda Bay. They crossed the buffalo plains of South Texas, passing the Nueces, San Antonio, and Guadalupe Rivers as they made their way again toward La Salle's lost colony.

"What I noticed," Father Massanet wrote, "was that on our first trip we had found many Indians along the rivers and everywhere else, while this time we went to inspect the Bay of Espíritu Santo [Matagorda Bay] and returned to the Guadalupe River without having found a single Indian in all the country."

Perhaps La Salle's colonists had unknowingly enacted a last revenge by planting smallpox among the Indians.

On April 26, 1690, Massanet and de León reached Fort St. Louis for the second time, and the priest noted, "I myself set fire to the fort, and as there was a high wind . . . in half an hour the fort was in ashes."

Then they again took up their journey, but this time they continued across the prairie toward the country of the "Texas" (Hasinai) Indians rather than returning right away to Mexico as they had done the year before.

Travel had become routine by this time. The horsemen in the caravan found it was easier to catch their mounts each morning and drive the cattle onward. Shortly after the middle of May they entered the country of the Hasinai Indians, as recounted in de León's journal:

Saturday, May 20th: Upon emerging from the wood we found a large valley which was named San Sebastian and at one side of

said valley we found four ranches of Indians who had planted
maize [corn] and frijoles [beans]. . . .

Monday, May 22nd: We set out northeast-by-east through some
groves of live-oak, crossing five dry arroyos and some small hills
where there are veins of black and red stone, and continued until
we reached a valley thickly settled with the houses of the Texas
[Hasinai] Indians. About them were fields of maize, beans,
pumpkins, and watermelons. . . . At about a quarter of a league
we found another valley of Texas Indians and their houses. . . .
To this settlement we gave the name of San Francisco de los
Tejas.

The Spaniards had arrived among the Hasinai along the Neches
and Angelina Rivers. They made no mention of seeing horses or cattle,
but the Hasinai must have had horses because La Salle had seen some
in the villages five years previous. Quickly de León and Father Massanet had the Hasinai build a church in which they could learn "the
mysteries of our holy Catholic faith." Soon de León made ready to return to Coahuila, and on the first day of June he, Massanet, and most
of the soldiers rode away, leaving behind three missionaries, a few soldiers, horses, cows, plows, axes, spades, and "other necessaries."

It turned out they also left something less necessary. A year after de
León's arrival, the Spanish Franciscan missionary Casañas would report that "about three thousand persons among all the friendly tribes
of the Tejias [Hasinai] must have died during the epidemic which the
Lord sent during the month of March, 1691." Such were the mysteries
of the holy faith.

Within a quarter century, "thousands of cows, bulls, horses, and
mares" roamed the countryside about the missions to the Hasinai.
Westward on the Trinity, travelers saw by this time "wild cattle lost by
the Spaniards on their first [de León's 1690] expedition into Texas."

In 1712 André Penicaut accompanied a party of Frenchmen from
lower Louisiana into the Hasinai country by way of the Mississippi
and Red Rivers. The flamboyant Louis Juchereau de Saint Denis of
Biloxi led the expedition, desiring to promote trading relations between the Spanish and French. The Frenchmen stopped briefly in the
Hasinai villages and then moved beyond the Hasinai country all the
way to Spanish settlements in Mexico. A few months later Penicaut re-

turned to the Angelina country to find the Hasinai warriors away. His diary entry shows how dependent on horses the Indians had become.

At the time we got there, very few savages were in their village: the others had gone away to wage war against another savage nation named the Kitaesches [Kichai tribe of the Caddo confederacy]. These savages make war quite differently from those along the bank of the Missicipy, for they all go on horseback, armed with a quiver made of buffalo hide, filled with arrows, which hangs slung over the shoulder behind their backs. They have a bow and in their left arm a small shield of buffalo hide with which they ward off arrows. . . .

From the Hasinai villages, Penicaut continued on toward Natchitoches in what is now Louisiana. Soon he met with another Caddo group, where he was reminded that cattle as well as horses had been in use for some time:

On our way back [to Natchitoches from the Hasinai villages] we passed through the village of the savages named the Yatacez [another Caddo tribe], whom we persuaded to come and live with us at the Nassitoches, where we conducted them together with their women and children and their cattle loaded with their grains and their personal belongings. . . .

Bellies that could turn the grass to human food and transportation had arrived to stay.

7   Off the End of a Gun

A well-regulated militia being necessary to the security of a free State, the right of the people to keep and bear arms shall not be infringed.

Constitution of the United States, Second Amendment

My brother and I measured life's progress in the early years by the stages in our acquisition of hunting weapons. Sticks dominated in preschool times, and in addition to making spears and clubs we fashioned bats to whack at bumblebees that hovered about the yard in summer. Stones leaped into prominence with our advance to slingshots; thereafter, we yearned for our parents to take us to the gravel pit dug by road repairmen so we could stuff our pockets with top-quality pebbles. After that, the shared BB gun briefly occupied center stage, but it quickly lost out to the single-shot .22 rifles that somehow made their way from the Sears Roebuck catalog to the space beneath our Christmas tree when Jack was ten and I was eleven.

As the grown-ups had adopted the new farming technology with its abridgements of independence, so we embraced each new and more powerful weapon with seldom a worry that its operation required supplies from outside. Only the sticks had been totally our own. Sling-shots needed elastic bands, which came first from the red tire tubes of natural rubber, next from the inferior black tubes that replaced the red ones in the late 1940s, and finally from boxes labeled "large rubber bands." BB's and .22 cartridges came in packets from the Western Auto hardware store, manufactured by an alchemy I never understood and seldom thought about. The store always had those things and would until eternity if you had the money to buy them.

The .22 rifles elevated us to the apex of youthful power. For fifty cents you could get a box of fifty "short" cartridges, the least powerful .22 ammunition available in Jasper but standard for birds and squirrels. From Corbett we found that shorts also were deadly on hogs if you placed the shot properly.

We lived in a hunter's coma until the first northers blew in fall and the robins arrived. Wave on wave the birds would come, from some unknown source in the north. They would swoop out of the frosty blue to infuse holly and yaupon trees with a teeming animal vigor.

"Chip! Tee-tee-tee-tee!"

Saturday morning would find us sneaking through a second-growth hardwood tangle with our .22's to get a bead on a russet breast. Robin pie for supper.

People said later we weren't supposed to shoot robins. Northern city dwellers waited each spring for them to return to sing songs we in the South had never heard and to run about the lawns eating earth-worms. When Texas skies emptied of robins in the late fifties and six-ties, I wondered whether we had killed them all. It was some relief to later learn there might have been other culprits — pesticides sprayed on northern lawns or southern hardwoods cut and replaced with loblolly pine.

≋The human body surpasses that of any other animal in its fitness for hurling objects. Early people everywhere found that casting sticks and stones could break bones and thereby aid them in hunting animals and defending themselves. Later, for thousands of years, spears tipped with stone or bone served as hunting implements. Invention of the throwing stick, or atlatl, and eventually the bow lent greater speed to spears and arrows, letting hunters kill at greater distances. Thus, as time went on, for men to compete successfully in hunts and battles depended more and more on their ability to send projectiles accurately and far.

When people in the Old World a thousand years or so after the birth of Christ found that certain chemical concoctions could explode, they marveled at the noise and flash. Some credit the Chinese for inventing gunpowder, but the Europeans or the Arabians may have equally valid claims. In any case, Friar Roger Bacon of England left one of the earliest proofs of such knowledge—just prior to A.D. 1250 he wrote down the formula for gunpowder. He was so frightened of its power that he concealed the formula for many years. But others knew about it also, and the genie got out of the bottle.

The properties of gunpowder when ignited, coupled with the fascination of men for hurling projectiles, soon led to the invention of guns. History indicates that the earliest ones resembled cannons; they thundered upon the European scene by A.D. 1300. By the time Queen Isabella and King Ferdinand sent Columbus on his way to America, European gunsmiths made hand-held cannons with trigger and match for setting off the powder. Improved forms of these early matchlocks armed European settlers in the New World from the mid-1500s to the mid-1600s. The flintlock, which ignited the powder with a flint instead of with a match, gradually replaced the matchlock and dominated as hand-held armament in the New World until the nineteenth century. The so-called musket, a shoulder firearm that changed over time from matchlock to flintlock and from heavy to light, decimated American Indians and wildlife from the sixteenth to the nineteenth centuries.

La Salle's colonists struck the Texas coast in 1684 armed with cannons, muskets, and other assorted firearms. Texas Indians at the time had no knowledge of guns, and firearms gave the settlers at Fort St. Louis great advantages, but these soon were compromised by sickness and general incompetence among the colonists. When Alonso de León and Father Massanet first reached the abandoned colony in the spring of 1689, they found, in addition to bodies and a cemetery, "more than a hundred stocks of flintlock arquebuses, without locks or barrels [and] . . . eight pieces of artillery. . . ."

The members of La Salle's party who eventually made their way back to Montreal survived by their guns. The travelers found that the Indians, if unfriendly, could generally be held at bay by the threat and superiority of firearms. Bison, deer, and other game, unaccustomed to death cast from such great distances, stood easy marks for the experienced hunter.

Indians probably coveted guns from the time they saw the power conveyed by this wondrous weapon. La Salle found among the Hasinai some friendly "ambassadors" from the Chouman (Jumano) tribe which lived southwest of the Hasinai and was "always at war with New Spain." One of these Indians tried to enlist the aid of La Salle in their war against the Spanish, according to Father Anastasius Douay's diary:

> He told us . . . that if we would go with them, or give them guns, they could easily conquer them [the Spanish] because they were a cowardly race, who had no courage, and made people walk before them with a fan to refresh them in hot weather.

The Spanish had been reluctant to put firearms into the hands of the natives. Perhaps there was good reason.

It would not be long after the Hasinai and their neighbors acquired horses and cows that they got guns as well. The interlude in which the Indians described by André Penicaut fought from horseback armed with quivers of arrows and buffalo hide shields was to be a brief one.

The superiority of firearms caused a revolution also in the hunting of animals. Historian Richard White quotes an early-nineteenth-century Mississippi Choctaw:

> [Guns] changed the nature of the hunt entirely. In place of the large companies and laborious running, surrounding, and driving, men would sneak out alone and could accomplish more than twenty men could with the bow and arrow. . . .

The French who passed through the Hasinai country in the early 1700s had a keen awareness of the utility of guns in frontier survival. Several times Penicaut described how he had to "live off the end of his gun." The French in general tended to demonstrate more compassion for the Indians' lack of firearms than did the Spanish and perhaps for this reason were the first to liberate the Hasinai from the bondage of the bow and arrow.

When Saint Denis paid a second visit to the Hasinai in November 1714, he bartered guns, beads, knives, and cloth for cattle and buffalo hides. In 1716 the Spaniard Domingo Ramón reported in dismay to his superiors that he had found among the Hasinai eighteen or twenty long arquebuses (early matchlocks) and other items of French origin: ". . . upon being asked where they secured all these things they said the French from Natchitoches brought them in square boats on the river and gave them to the Indians for horses and skins of animals."

By this time, Indians throughout most of the southeastern United States had acquired firearms and knew how to use them. Guns had become valued trade items. Often the Spanish, French, or English armed Indians as allies against other Europeans in America or other Indians.

Replacing the primitive weapons of the southern Indians with firearms caused the numbers of larger animals to plummet. Sharp declines in the Indian populations during the early eighteenth century, from a new wave of European diseases as well as from intertribal slave raids and warfare, might have introduced a brief respite, but the escalating trade in deerskins and other hides had encouraged hunters armed with guns to penetrate all regions east of the Mississippi. Shortly, the bark of muskets would intensify in Texas.

I did not fully appreciate the superiority of firearms over archery until after some years of experimentation making and using bows and arrows. I still have not entirely abandoned that romantic pursuit. But now I know how the Indians and deer must have felt when they first ran into men with guns.

The major problem with the bow and arrow is the difficulty in hitting a distant target. Beyond forty yards, even with high-tech equipment, an arrow's arc becomes so pronounced that a misjudgment of the range by five yards will send the shaft over or under a deer-sized target. Beyond sixty yards, forget effective hunting, even if you're the national champ with the best modern bow. That Native Americans consistently bagged deer with handmade bows and arrows speaks highly of their predatory skills.

By contrast, even the muskets of La Salle's day killed deer and people out to a hundred yards or so, and consistently. Increasing a projectile's effective range from forty yards to a hundred yards increases the area under command by six times. Further, getting within archery range of an animal takes infinitely more patience and skill than getting within musket range.

Once a hunting partner of mine, whose name I will withhold to preserve his reputation, lashed a homemade but sharp obsidian arrowhead to the tip of a hunting arrow and went in quest of javelina. These little pigs of the Southwest make fine quarry for the bowhunter, for they seem almost blind to a human standing motionless. After a few days of hunting, he got his chance — a pig walked by at twenty paces. Drawing his sixty-pound-pull fiberglass bow to its fullest, he released the arrow straight and true. It struck the animal amidships — and bounced off. The pig ran away.

Hats off to the Indian with the bow and arrow who met the white man with the musket. I, too, would have traded anything to get my hands on that wondrous weapon.

I have not shot a robin in many years. Today in New Mexico, robins nest in the backyard apple tree and feed on worms in the garden. I hear them sing the song the Yankees heard when I was young.

Once more in the fall I see flocks of them arrive. In this arid country they feed on juniper berries instead of holly.

"Chip! Tee-tee-tee-tee!"

Once more the circle has come round.

The utmost good faith shall always be observed towards the Indians;
their lands and property shall never be taken from them without
their consent; and, in their property, rights, and liberty, they shall
never be invaded or disturbed, unless in just and lawful wars
authorized by Congress. . . .

U.S. Government, Northwest Ordinance, 1787, Article 3

Before my brother and I started school, we lived for a while in a one-room cabin a hundred yards or so from Pa Graham's house. Because Daddy shipped out periodically with the ocean-going transport system called the merchant marines, it made sense for Mama and us kids to live next door to a family support system.

At Pa Graham's, the only dependable water came from a cistern that caught rainfall runoff from the cypress-shingle roof. In wet years they got additional water from a well with a hand pump in the backyard. Doing laundry took a lot of water, so on clothes-washing days Nama and Mama usually carted the dirty overalls, dresses, and bed sheets a half mile down the hill to a place called Delaney Spring. While they washed, Jack and I played in the water of a little rivulet that originated from the spring.

Corbett showed Jack and me a special place nearby. A long-gone railroad he referred to as the Kirby Main Line had gouged a trench through the high ground near the stream. Rain had eroded the soil. Sometimes, if you looked long enough among the sand jack leaves and pine needles, you could find a railroad spike. But what we usually looked for when we went there were flint arrowheads.

Soon we assembled a small collection of points. Most ranged from an inch to two inches long, and many of these were so misshapen we speculated kids had made them. But there also were the delicate "bird" points, and sometimes larger ones, that approached perfection.

One of these showed to kids at school brought a great deal more prestige than an "A" on your report card. Marbles could not buy them.

At first the points seemed little more than rippled stone with the arrowhead shape, detached from all meaning other than the value built by their scarcity and by commentary from adults. Then came the time when a particularly sharp-edged one grew an imaginary feathered shaft attached by sinew. Then a bow appeared, held by a make-believe human with Anglo features stained dark like the men in the Broken Arrow movie.

About this time, the name Indian Creek, an always clear and mossy stream that headed up a mile or so east of Pa Graham's, also took on new meaning. Open pinewoods plunged into sweet bay cypress marsh at the edge of Indian Creek bottom, and we swam in an ice-cold pool downstream where the creek crossed the farm-to-market road into town. But I never found any arrowheads anywhere along the creek; the ground was too thick with ferns and leaves.

"Did you ever see an Indian?" I asked Corbett one day when further enlightenment had become stymied by lack of information.

"One came by once, a long time ago," he said. "Your Nama fixed him some food, and he traveled on."

That got me to wondering what had happened to the Indians. It was many years and books later that I found out.

On Friday, June 1, 1690, the de León and Massanet expedition, after having spent less than two weeks in the Angelina country, set out on their return to Mexico. They left behind the seeds of the first European colony to be planted among the Hasinai. They took with them four relatives of the chief; these, according to Massanet, were to "bring back numerous presents" from Mexico to the Hasinai.

Either on this trip or another soon thereafter, a young Indian girl made the journey from the shady village of the Hasinai to the shimmering heat of Mexico. Exactly when she made the trip and how old she was remain hidden by the cloak of time. Spanish chroniclers refer to her only later, after she had moved back to her people: "[She] had been baptized and reared in the mission of San Juan Batiste, on the Rio Grande, in Coahuila [and] . . . having returned to her country, proved very useful to the Spaniards because of her knowledge of the language and her good services in winning the goodwill of her people for the Spaniards."

The Spanish people called her Angelina. This they also named the river from which she had come and to which she returned. In 1712 she had acted as translator for the Spanish-speaking Frenchman Saint Denis when he and André Penicaut passed through her village. In 1720 she befriended a Frenchman named Belle-Isle who entered her land; at his departure, she sent her two sons to guide him back to Louisiana. In 1721 she turned up on the Trinity River at the Camino Real (now Highway 21) crossing with three other Hasinai women and several chiefs, to meet with Aguayo, the governor of Coahuila, and Saint Denis. There is no record of how much longer she lived or where she died.

No one knows how many of Angelina's people lived before Columbus's time in what is now eastern Texas. Inhabitants of the entire southeastern United States may have numbered in the millions. Chroniclers of the Hernando de Soto expedition of 1539–1543, the first major European trek through the South, described people of the Choctaw nation, Mississippi, as living cheek to jowl on cultivated land along the river terraces.

Like European settlers, the Indian farmers before them had hunted in the hinterlands, among the pinehills and flatlands where soils were poor. Some think it likely that, despite the limitations of the bow and arrow, they often overhunted choice game. The early Choctaws told of killing off the deer near settlements and moving far afield in search of more.

Europeans traveling through the southern countryside a century and a half to two centuries after de Soto met with Indian fields and orchards strangely vacant, overgrown with briars and brush. Diseases introduced by de Soto and others of his time had swept through the farming Indians. Some fared worse than others.

An incident that happened centuries later indicates the magnitude of death that the earliest epidemics could have caused. This time, a man who knew of germs and had an urge to write was there.

Charlie Brower told the story. The places were Barrow and the nearby Utkiavie village at farthest north Alaska. The time was near the turning of the nineteenth to the twentieth century.

The inland Eskimos had come to trade. These hunters of the caribou had seldom met a white person. While they camped near Barrow, whaling ships arrived with men who brought ashore their whiskey for a party.

Several days later, Barrow residents, whites as well as coastal Eskimos who had met with whaling ships and sailors many times before, caught a kind of flu. Eventually it killed a few of them, but nearly all recovered.

When Charlie Brower went to see about the inland Eskimos camped outside Barrow, he found beginnings of a different story. Some had taken very sick, and their "devil-doctors" had urged them all into their boats to head for home.

Soon afterward, an Eskimo who had not heard about the sickness stopped at Barrow to tell of people lying dead along the river route followed by the fleeing people. When Brower heard this, he and a crew of men set out. He later wrote a story that may have happened many times before in lands that lay to the south:

Following the homeward course of the stricken people we came to the first evidence of disaster not ten miles away — a woman with a young baby. She had died on the bank of the lagoon. The child had lived a while longer. Its body lay quite a way off.

The farther we went, the greater grew the tragedy. It was clear that from the day they set out for home in their oomiaks [skin boats] they had been dying all along the coast and up the rivers. From the postures of the bodies, we could almost visualize it happening — the stronger members dragging the weaker onto the banks to die, then paddling a little farther until it came their turn to be abandoned.

I never shall forget one camp we came to, with its three empty boats and a dozen bodies sprawled around on the bank. Men, women, children — all as cold as the ashes of the fire they'd tried hard to build. And off at one side a string of turquoise beads that would have brought a fortune a few years before.

From there we turned back, realizing that what we had seen was only a sample of what lay farther back along the remote inland waterways.

All that fall and the next summer we kept getting reports from hunters of bodies discovered along far river banks, sometimes alone, sometimes with a few belongings scattered around.

It is my opinion that of those two hundred or more husky inland Eskimos who so light-heartedly danced with us at Utkiavie, not one was left alive.

In Angelina's time, the Hasinai, despite past diseases, still numbered in the thousands. Corn and other crops probably provided the primary sustenance. When the Frenchman Joutel came among them, at the time Angelina would have been a child, he wrote:

> [The women] . . . do the greater part of the [soil cultivation]. . . . The day being appointed, all those who are informed come to work with a kind of mattock which some make of a buffalo bone and others of a piece of wood fastened with cords made of tree bark. . . . If [a man] comes back from the hunt with venison, it supplies the [noontime] feast; if they have none, they cook corn in the ashes or boil it with Brazil beans. . . . After this repast most of them amuse themselves for the rest of the day. . . . These savages have no utensil of iron, and . . . they can only scratch the earth, not being able to open it very deep; however, things grow there wonderfully well.

Writing shortly afterward, Fray Isidro Felix Espinoza noted that the Hasinai also harvested the bounty of the native trees and vines:

> They gather quantities of thick-shelled nuts and acorns to last a whole year. . . . In addition to the nut-bearing trees, there are other fruit trees, like the medlar [probably hawthorn], the plum, and the large wild cherry. . . . There are great quantities of red and white mulberries and large blackberries which are very sweet. . . .

Espinoza also found them harvesting fish from the streams and lakes:

There are many lagoons [ox-bow lakes along the rivers] in which an abundance of fish are found. These fish are not always found in the same spots, but the locations vary according to the rises in the rivers and arroyos during the winter. When warm weather comes the Indians go with their families to certain spots and stay for some days, living on fish. They carry home quantities of cooked fish. . . .

Espinoza told about their hunts for deer, buffalo, and bear:

Before they go out to hunt deer, they put on a post in their thatched huts the dry head of a deer including the neck and horns, which they pray to their caddi ayo that he will put the prey into their hands. . . . They [then] put its [the deer's] head at the door of the hut and with another just like it they go out into the woods to hunt, covering their naked bodies with white dirt. When they have killed a deer, they divide the animal. For some time they talk into its ear but I do not know the meaning of this puzzle. . . .

The buffalo is distant more than forty leagues from the Texas [Hasinai] country, and [to hunt them] . . . the Indians go well armed because at this time if they fall in with the Apaches the two murder each other unmercifully. At this time, which is usually in the winter, they are accustomed to kill a great number of bears. . . . These bears live on nuts and acorns which abound in this country.

While the Spaniards watched the Hasinai grow corn and gather wild food as they probably had for centuries, an ominous storm brewed a thousand miles toward the east. It seethed among the swelling ranks of English-speaking peoples who had come across the sea with a mighty thirst for land. These people listened to a different "caddi ayo," and most of them would have thought that talking to a dead deer showed some heathen madness.

Already they were pushing westward. They were very good at learning how to cope with tangled forests, swollen rivers, and stubborn Indians. They sent traders out to open up the way, and eventually the traders perfected a strategy that worked.

First, they found trading partners among the Indian tribes, offering axes, knives, pots, kettles, and guns for furs and deerskins. Over time the Indians grew dependent on these things that made life so much easier. They needed guns, especially, to get more deerskins and to put them on an equal footing with any hostile Indian neighbors.

The white traders instituted credit systems, through which the unsuspecting Indians built up debts. Running out of skins and lacking other means to pay, the tribal leaders started ceding tribal lands to settle what they owed to traders.

White settlers moved into the newly claimed lands adjacent to the Indians. Land disputes developed. The Europeans by now held the upper hand in terms of weaponry and numbers, and the Indians usually lost in these disputes. The countryside over which the Indians hunted shrank, as did the numbers of deer and other game. More and more the only thing the Indians had to trade was land.

As tribal lands shrank, so did the Indian numbers. New waves of disease swept through villages. The tribes skirmished frequently among themselves and with the Europeans. But despite the rapid dwindling of the Indian numbers and the lands they claimed, the whites became impatient.

The American Revolution ended in 1783, and colonists began pushing more eagerly westward. In the 1830s President Andrew Jackson sent in the clean-up crew — he marched most of the remaining southern Indian tribes to beyond the Mississippi in a process called removal. Angelina's people faded like their southern cousins, though they lasted longer because the Spanish had kept the English-speaking hordes at bay across the Sabine River until 1821.

No one had ever counted the Hasinai in Angelina's time. A Canadian who had lived among them in 1699 guessed the warriors among them numbered six or seven hundred, and a guess in 1716 by Diego Ramón set the total number at four to five thousand. By 1780, according to the Spaniards, the Hasinai might have numbered as few as one thousand.

Following Mexico's opening of Texas to Americans in 1821, the Hasinai began to move about under pressure from the Anglos. Their intermarriages with whites and with Indians from other tribes complicated attempts to determine their status. In 1828 José María Sanchez visited their Angelina homeland and, despite the influx of Americans that had come into the country, he found a band of Hasinai a few miles from the river, along with remnants of other tribes that had come from farther east under pressure from the whites:

> ... we found some houses, or huts, a camp of Nacogdochitos [Hasinai] Indians, a peaceful tribe. They [the men] were in the greatest inaction, while the women worked the fields with the greatest fatigue in this burning climate to maintain their tyrants. . . . While crossing a fairly large creek called El Loco, we saw other huts of Tejas [Hasinai] Indians where we witnessed the same tyrannical scenes as in the village of the Nacogdochitos.
>
> Different tribes of Indians such as the Tejas, Nadacos, Hguanes, Savanos, Cherokees, Kickapoos, Delawares, Cutchates, Alabamas, Quichas, and Cados, continually enter Nacagdoches, but they are all peaceful and carry on their trade in the city with skins, corn, pumpkins, and beans. These tribes are located in the neighborhood of Nacagdoches, their Pueblos being intermingled with the settlements of the Americans who are scattered throughout Texas.

The increased influx of Americans seeking land after the Texas Americans gained their independence from Mexico in 1836 pushed the Indians even farther westward. Individuals among the remaining Hasinai had no tradition to stake out and claim units of land and probably would have found little opportunity in any case. In 1846, after Texas took the plunge from republic to statehood, Robert S. Neighbors, the U.S. government's special commissioner to the Texas Indians, reported a group of Hasinai living a hundred miles west of the Angelina country with two related Caddo groups "forty-five miles from Torrey's trading house" on the Brazos River.

In 1855 the U.S. government set aside 37,152 acres on "the main fork of the Brazos River, about twelve or fifteen miles south of Fort Belknap" as a reservation for the Caddoes (including Hasinai) plus groups of Waco, Tawakoni, Kichai, Tonkawa, and some Delaware Indians.

Commissioner Neighbors reported to the acting commissioner of Indian Affairs in September of that year: "They are now settled on this reservation, as you will perceive by reference to the census rolls herewith enclosed, 794 Indians of the following tribes, to wit: 205 Anadahkos, 188 Caddoes, 136 Tahwaclorroes [Tawakoni], 94 Wacos, and 171 Tonkahwas."

By 1858 Anglo Texans coveted even this reservation. Local settlers trumped up grievances against the Indians. Two days after Christmas, a group of whites attacked seventeen Indian men, women, and children encamped in a bend of the Brazos near the mouth of Keechi Creek, killing "seven of the best and most inoffensive Indians on the reserve." The next year the federal government removed all Indians on the reserve northward to the Witchita Indian agency in what is now Oklahoma. There the agents herded them together with the other southern tribes. In 1880 the American Indian Office estimated there were thirty Hasinai left in Oklahoma. But, given the normal tendency for mating urges to frustrate the best intentions and estimates of sociologists and politicians, their genes may by that time have stretched from coast to coast and sent a spirit born of shaded forests to enrich the heritage of many Europeans.

A 1991 National Geographic map entitled "Native American Heritage" shows tiny dots of Indian reservation lands remaining in the southern states. Several are in Florida and one each in Texas, Mississippi, and North Carolina; none appear elsewhere. This depiction omits a few small reservations and fails to show that some Indians live off reservations, but its message is clear — not many Indians remain.

The tract of Indian land in Texas is not Hasinai. The Rand McNally highway map shows it as a series of small connected blocks of land near State Highway 190 between Woodville and Livingston. Signs beside the highway mark the exit to the village: "Tours, Camping, Restrooms." A granite marker standing in the Y of the turn-off says:

> Alabama and Coushatti Indians
> who came into Texas
> early in the nineteenth
> century and have always
> been friendly with the whites.

There is no marker that I know of for the grave of Angelina or for others of her people. Her descendants boast no genealogy to tell them who they are. But almost like an afterthought, someone raised her name in metal on a sign where Texas Highway 21 takes cars and trucks across her river.

☙Southern people of European descent put a lot of stock in ancestry. A common hobby among older people is to track the family name back for generations, showing friends and relatives photos of great-grandfather John who fought in the Civil War or the letters from great-aunt Lucy who married a millionaire. A good lineage is a great comfort.

My mother has worked for years on a family tree. "I believe in telling it like it was," she says, "but it's odd how some people working on genealogies conveniently forget that their Uncle George went to jail for shooting a man or can't figure out how to deal with illegitimate children and common-law marriages."

Nearly all agree that Indian blood is a good thing to have in the family. It is not quite as clear that people thought it a good thing at the time it made its entry.

"A Choctaw man several generations back on your daddy's side makes you one-sixteenth Indian," my mother has often told me, and I take a great deal of comfort in that. "But shortly after the birth of his first child," she sometimes adds, "they found him drowned in the river. Nobody ever wrote down how it happened."

In my seventh and eighth grades, we had a good basketball team. We sometimes loaded on the school bus and traveled the sixty miles or so to "Big Sandy" to play the Alabama-Coushatti Indians. They nearly always beat us. By any measure, they were good at basketball.

But we would sometimes get mad when we thought they didn't play by the rules. Occasionally, from out of nowhere, a hand would reach to hold your arm just before a lay-up, and the referees would never see it.

That was back when my teachers and history books said real Americans had come from European ancestry and that they always had played fair.

I'm bound to follow the longhorn cow,
Wherever the critter goes. . . .
Traditional cowboy song

I never thought of Pa Graham as a cowboy. He was too old, for one thing, and I couldn't imagine him wearing a wide-brimmed hat or spurs. Besides, cowboys inhabited prairies and mountains, not forests, and they rode their horses fast. I can't recall ever having seen Pa astride a horse.

That old saddle hanging from the log wall of his corncrib bore little resemblance to the ones Randolph Scott used. I remember it as a dusty assemblage of cracked leather. Its skirts had curled from moisture and disuse to expose the wooden tree beneath. The perforated steel stirrups had rusted in the humid air, and the pommel of the horn, likewise metal, stared at me with twin holes that looked like the end of a pig's snout.

Corbett's preoccupation with stock might have given me a hint about Pa's earlier life, had I been old enough to know about tradition. Large dogs of mixed breeding that followed Corbett when he rode away on Dan or Stepper seemed always to be around. On occasion the log corrals down by the corncrib would fill with bawling cattle. The grown-ups told a lot of cow stories to each other.

"Remember the time that long-horn cow chased old G. W. Warner over the cowpen fence? . . ."

Some of the English-speaking colonists who came to America brought cattle and a cattle-herding life-style with them from England, Scotland, and Ireland, says Terry Jordan, historical geographer at the University of Texas. Grazing cattle on unfenced range had been tradition for centuries in the highlands of the British Isles. As descendants of these early European colonists settled along the eastern seaboard, they modified old cattle-herding practices to fit the new frontier.

For a century and a half after they settled in the New World, English-speaking folk hovered at the eastern edge of the southern woods. In this time, they built a way of life that worked: they learned which trees to use for what, which animals to hunt and how, which crops to plant and when, and how to herd stock. Their populations grew. When the obstacles built by Indians and by French and Spanish kings fell down, the English traveled west.

What worked in Carolina worked also in Alabama and Mississippi. As Anglos pushed the frontier ever westward, they left behind a trail of worn-out relatives on worn-out farms, fewer deer and turkeys than they had found at first, and wild woods hogs and cows to take the place of game. They used land up without much thought; there was always more, farther on.

Plain folk far outnumbered those of wealth and social standing in the movement west. They clung to the edges of the pinelands and the hills. Most possessed a hickory-tough resilience born of little baggage — a horse or two, a few cows, a bunch of hogs, and farming tools. Scottish and Irish names abounded among them.

They looked for places where a modest piece of fertile ground abutted on the pinelands. There they nested, with their gardens in the darker soil and their hogs and cattle ranging in the pinelands and the swamps. Oftentimes the simple fact of neighbors crowding in beside them was enough to make them hitch their team and move on farther west, to look for elbow room at another garden spot beside the pine-woods "barrens."

When these immigrants reached Texas, they bumped into a culture that glorified the cow. Before, to most of them, cattle had offered milk and meat to supplement cotton, corn, and beans. Now the vastness of the range and the Spanish notion of a life-style free from working land from dawn to dusk introduced a different drummer.

Pa Graham's father, Isaac Nelson Graham, came from common stock of Scot and Irish blood. Born on Alabama soil in 1825 on the crest of westward movement, he did not tarry long when he got old enough to travel. The age of twenty found him farther down the road, in Jones County, Mississippi, married to Lavina Parker and the father of a baby daughter.

Isaac and Lavina stayed in Mississippi long enough to see a decade pass and three more children come. Then they loaded up the wagon. Isaac gathered his few cattle and the hogs that he could drive and called the dogs. They set a course for Texas, where the opportunities were better, people said. Lavina kept her eyes straight ahead between the mules and tried not to think of anything but how to keep the wagon wheels from missing all the holes in the road.

Just before the War between the States caught fire, the Grahams crossed the Sabine River into Texas at the place where Texas Highway 63 now meets Louisiana Highway 8. For some time they had been following a wagon road people called the Beef Trail. A week later and fifty miles farther westward on the Beef Trail road, they stepped off a ferry and shortly pulled into the town of De Zavala, on a rise near the east bank of the Angelina.

The children peered out from the wagon cover. They saw scattered houses made of logs, chickens scratching in the dirt, and trees that looked like those back home. Here the Grahams stopped, to add their numbers to the forty families there already.

The village had been named for Lorenzo de Zavala, impresario from Mexico, who had left the Spanish camp and joined the Anglos when the Texas Revolution came in 1836. A Thomas Huling owned the De Zavala townsite after 1836, but in 1847 he sold it to an Englishman in London for five thousand boxes of Green Mountain Ointment and its recipe. People later called the village just Zavala, and later still, Old Zavala, for a new place called Zavalla grew up twenty miles northwestward as the original Zavala disappeared.

In this tiny town beside the Angelina River, Lavina bore three more children. The last, born in mid-September 1868, is listed in the record books as David Henry; his family called him Henry. We called him Pa.

Lavina died three days later. In De Zavala at that time of year, the autumn northers might have started, bringing coolness. Within a month the black gum leaves would start to bleed against the stubborn green of summer.

Necessity lent an urgent tone to courtship in those days. Length of mourning shortened when a man had a baby in the house and hungry mouths to feed. Within a year, Isaac had found himself another wife.

Isaac and the other settlers at the edge of the piney woods found a paradise for growing cattle. Solomon Alexander Wright, a neighbor forty miles southward, would later recollect his family's situation in a similar type of country, though less hilly:

> It was the most ideal location for a cow ranch imaginable. . . . Our range . . . comprised about eighty thousand acres, the west half slightly rolling, longleaf pinewoods, the east half marshes, alternating with strips of level pinewoods and numerous small swamps. . . . The pinewoods were perfectly open, without underbrush. . . .

Throughout the South for many years, the Grahams and families like them had been running livestock at the edges of the pinelands. Here, ordinary southern folk found a niche where wealthy planters did not come. The pinewood soils had not enough fertility for market crops. But they proved entirely adequate for stock.

By early in the nineteenth century, East Texas cattle had become a market item. In 1834 one William Wilson, a rancher near Galveston, had driven five-dollar cows to Louisiana, where they sold for thirty-five. Later, in the 1850s, pinelands ranchers had begun sending herds west as well, to stock the central Texas country. As had always been the case with goods for market, people selling cows learned to take them to a place where they were scarce.

Following the Civil War, during David Henry's childhood, the cattle business prospered and the drives to market grew to legendary stature. East Texas served not only as a source for stock but also as a passageway for cattle moving through. The Graham family often saw the drovers passing De Zavala.

Cattle following the Beef Trail went mostly to Louisiana shipping points. Coming from the west, they crossed at Jordan's Ferry on the

Neches and then at De Zavala on the Angelina. Moving farther east, they crossed the Sabine into Louisiana at Burr's Ferry or sometimes upstream a bit at Hadden's Ferry. Many clattered onto steamboats at the town of Alexandria on the Red River to travel down the Red to the Mississippi and to New Orleans, and thence to Yankee dining rooms.

Pens to hold the cattle stood at points along the trail, but often drovers simply held the cows at night by "riding herd." Solomon Wright recalled one such "unforgettable night" in his youth:

> Mother and my sisters stayed up all night and cooked, and the boys [riding herd] would come to the house in relays of two or three to get water, coffee, and lunch. The next morning, after they turned them [the cattle] out and started to Louisiana with them, us kids went down to the pasture to see what the ground looked like. There wasn't a blade of grass to be seen . . . where the day before the grass had been as high as a cow's back.

By the time Henry Graham knew the value of a dollar, cattle represented money to a backwoods Texas homestead. Few herdsmen made it rich — cows got lost during drives or caught the Texas cattle fever, tempers of the market changed, and there were limits to the land that individuals controlled. But ranching built a way of living that satisfied the souls of these Texas men, whose forebears had been chasing hairy beasts perhaps all the way back to the Pleistocene.

Henry's father, Isaac, had brought with him to Texas a southern way of tending cattle. Burn the grass in spring to start the green-up early. Ride amongst the cows from time to time and throw a little corn around to keep them tame. Drive them to the bottoms in the winter, if you can, so they can feed on switch cane.

In Texas, Mexican herders of Spanish origin taught the Anglo colonists a thing or two. The Spaniards had been herders since before Columbus, first in Spain and then in Mexico and Texas. They had built a cattle culture of their own. When the Texas Revolution ended and the flag of Mexico moved out, some Mexicans stayed in eastern Texas. One observer of the times noted, "Everyone acknowledges their skill with cattle, horses, and the other stock."

As Henry Graham grew to manhood, he learned cattle from this blend of cultures. He could build a bull-tight cowpen, ride a horse, rope a cow, and use his dogs to find the wild ones in the thickets. He al-

Don't fence me in. Henry "Pa" Graham at home in Peachtree about 1937. By this time the cattle drives past his home were only a memory.

ways kept a sharpened pocketknife to mend a broken saddle or to turn a bull into a steer at branding time.

In 1892 at the age of twenty-four, Henry married Mary Jane Ragan. The marriage might have taken place in Jasper, then the county seat, for Old Zavala by that time had lost its status as a town.

In those days fecundity rode frontier families like a yoke. When a year had passed, children started coming to the Graham household, and they kept it up for ten more years, just like clockwork, a new child every other year. By 1903, Henry and Mary Jane may have tired a bit; neighbors counted four years each between the last two children.

R. L., the second child, was born in 1895. His brothers later said he turned out to be a scrawny kid, defending himself against bigger boys with clenched fists. So they called him Corbett, fitting for a scrapper in the days of that famous boxer Jim Corbett and easier to yell than R. L.

Corbett grew from child to young man beside the Beef Trail in the first decade of the twentieth century. Saw and axe stayed busy at the edges of the settlement, and Zavala people made some spending money sending logs down the Angelina to the Neches and on to Beaumont near the coast. But getting logs to riverside proved always troublesome away from slough and settlement, and Corbett saw the uncut miles of oaks and hickories in the bottomland continue to give up their mast in fall by countless bushels. In the uplands, loggers had barely scratched the surface of the open stands of longleaf pine.

He learned to read and write and add at the Ebenezer school across the river. When the teacher held a session, Corbett and the other kids would daily ride the boat across and walk to where the schoolhouse stood. Floods from time to time would interrupt his schooling, and after several years he quit entirely to help the family make a living.

The land provided nearly all they needed. It gave them wood for house, barn, winter fires, and split-rail fences. It supported black-eyed peas and corn in summer gardens and fed their cows and hogs all year. From the woodlands came their venison and squirrel stew and from the river, catfish.

Also from the land came cash. The settlers sent logs and bales of cotton by river to the coastal marketplace and cows by hoof to shipping points. Money came back, to spend for axes, saws, plows, factory-made cloth, salt, and flour.

Corbett learned to fell a tree where he wanted it to fall. He learned to fashion implements from wood and scraps of iron. He helped plant the fields in spring, harvest the garden in summer, and put up food for winter.

He worked around the homeplace because he had to, but he loved to roam the woods and work with cows and hogs. The limits of his wanderings were set by how far he could walk or ride a horse. Few fences blocked the way, especially in the pinelands. From an open hilltop he could see the dust of cattle coming in from somewhere else and bound for yet another place.

There was so much space.

That is the land of lost content,
I see it shining plain,
The happy highways where I went
And cannot come again.
A. E. Housman, "Yon Far Country"

In 1905 Corbett's father, Pa Graham, got the itch. Uncle Hardy Parker's letters set it off. It festered, and Pa grew so restless that his wife, Mary Jane, or Jennie, knew he'd have to scratch it.

Uncle Hardy was the brother of Pa's long-dead mother, Lavina. Years earlier, he had moved from Mississippi and settled down in the Angelina country near the Grahams' home in De Zavala. Eventually he had moved on farther west, "for his health." He ended up in Rising Star, in a drier land beyond the woodlands, three hundred miles west of De Zavala and two days past Comanche.

As is common for a folk newly settled in a land thought satisfactory, he wrote letters home about the wondrous country he had found. Pa Graham read the letters.

All his thirty-seven years of life Pa Graham had spent living in the Angelina country. He had seen the dusty cowboys bring the herds in from the west, smelling of a land with far horizons. He had watched newcomers from farther east push into the countryside about the Angelina. Married couples added ten where two had been before. Of late it seemed he bumped into a person everywhere he turned. Worst of all, a railroad line had just been laid through the Angelina country; he could hear the whistle as the train approached De Zavala.

One-hundred-sixty-acre homesteads could be had near Rising Star, Uncle Parker said. All you had to do to own the land was stay on it for three years. The soil was good for farming and the settlers scarce.

Pa Graham bought a canvas cover for the wagon. He patched the harnesses and fattened up the mules. He helped the other Grahams plow their fields one last time, sold his land, and in a barn belonging to a relative packed the furniture and other heavy things that he and Jennie owned. As summer neared its end, they headed out for Rising Star.

Two mules pulled the wagon. Corbett and the other children slept each night on a mattress in the wagon bed. Pa Graham and Mama Jennie slept on pallets on the ground.

First, the family went northwest to Lufkin. From there they traveled west to ford the Neches River, smaller than it was straight west of De Zavala. Dutch oven biscuits from the sack of flour in the wagon fed them morning, noon, and night. Cookies, preserves, and salt bacon from home, and probably rabbits and squirrels shot along the road, added to the fare. They bought milk from farmers on the way.

"Risin' Star, you say? Well, if I was you, I'd head west to Crockett, then to Waco. Ask along the way."

Beyond Crockett, they crossed the Trinity River on a wooden bridge. Wagons moving westward had multiplied in recent years, and a road above the water could handle much more traffic than a ferry. When they reached Waco, they could hardly believe their eyes — an iron bridge spanned the Brazos.

Corbett's eyes grew even larger at the many buildings packed along the streets of Waco. Seeing all the horses, buggies, wagons, and crowds of people kept his bare feet rooted to the street.

An unfamiliar sound pulled the mules' ears like a magnet. The animals shuffled nervously in their harnesses. Corbett climbed up on the wagon seat to get a look. A shiny black contraption puttered past, without a horse to pull it, and everybody stared.

One more river to cross. Bohler's Ferry on the Angelina about 1922, near the present-day crossing of State Highway 63, a few miles downstream from Corbett's birthplace. Donated to the Jasper County Historical Commission by Jimmy Tanner.

"Must be one of them automobiles," Pa Graham said. Corbett rubbed his eyes.

Waco fell behind. At Valley Mills, the mules pulled the wagon through the shallow Bosque River. Farther on, they crossed the Leon River on a wooden bridge. Finally they reached Comanche.

The country had grown more open. It hadn't been too long, people said, since the Indians had made travel risky in these parts. By the time the Grahams pulled into the tiny town of Rising Star, they had been two weeks on the road.

Uncle Parker's family lived two miles out in a big white house. The weary travelers slept in beds again. Pa Graham started out to look for land. Two days later he fell sick.

The malaria attacks made him sweat a while and freeze a while. He thought he might die and vowed to go back home should he get well. Doubtless Jennie missed her family, too, and between them by this time they might have had enough of far horizons. Pa Graham did recover, and in late October they packed up and started back.

The sky clouded over, and the rain arrived. Day after day the wagon wheels rolled through mud; night after sleepless night the misty rain continued. Temporary pleasures came when a farmer let them cook a meal inside his kitchen and when a vacant church kept them dry one night.

Despite the rain, or perhaps because of it, they made this trip more quickly than the last. About midnight ten days after leaving Rising Star, they pulled in sight of Graham houses looming dark in the stump-dotted clearing. Dogs barked, and the mules brayed. Pa Graham gave a mighty yell, and kerosene lamps came on.

The children swarmed inside. Someone built a fire, and Corbett moved up near the hearth to warm his tired feet. They had bumped against their last frontier, and they were back.

Pa Graham tried to bargain for the land he'd sold, but the new owner showed no interest. Perhaps he thought it worth more now that the railroad seemed set to boost the lumbering economy. Forced to look elsewhere, Pa found a fifty-acre piece of ground ten miles eastward down the Kirby Main Line, as they called the new railroad.

This new piece of ground still had elbow room. Hemmed in by the piney woods, it straddled a divide. Here and there on ridges, oak and hickory indicated sandy loam where a man could likely grow a crop. Mostly though, the soil seemed poor enough to make ambitious farmers shun the neighborhood.

The land lay north a half mile from the railroad line. Pa Graham started on a house beneath the red oaks on a hill.

He knew this country well from years of riding it to look for cows and hogs when he had lived in De Zavala. When he looked north and west from the highest hill, he could see the Angelina lowlands in the distance. Woods in that direction showed the tracks of raccoons, hogs, and deer but not much sign of people till you reached the river.

Eastward rolled the sterile pinelands, mile on mile, following the Kirby track. Only southward, where a mile away from Pa's land the pinewoods graded into Peachtree's hardwood hammock land, did the soil seem really good for farming.

Corbett grew beyond the age of ten at this homeplace on the northern fringe of Peachtree, about ten miles northwest of Jasper. Open pinelands with miles of grass rolled across the hills. Hickory trees and oaks — red, blackjack, sand jack — stood on crests of sandy ridges. Hillside springs gave rise to baygall thickets near the heads of pinewoods streams, which trickled down the sandy slopes between the ridges, supporting hardwood stringers choked with bay, magnolia, beech, and ironwood trees. Lower down, the stringers met the bigger bottomlands.

As Corbett grew, he saw the cows and hogs put to best advantage the diversity of land. Cattle grazed the grasses in the piney woods from spring to fall but sought out upland baygalls or switch cane bottoms in the winter. Woods hogs found the wettest sites in spring; they came to acorns, hickory nuts, and other hardwood mast in summer, fall, and winter.

Wild animals likewise thrived, where hunters let them. Bears had once fed alongside hogs and on them, but by Corbett's youth they were nearly gone. Deer and turkeys liked the grassland edges when the grasshoppers, grass seed-heads, and greenery were at their peak but, like the hogs, looked for hardwood mast when and where it fell. Gray squirrels swarmed in bottomlands and hammocks, living in a small home range and switching diet from beech to oak to magnolia to hickory as the seasons changed. Fox squirrels roamed more widely in the open woods, moving from the seeds of longleaf uplands to the mast of hardwood stringers as required to find their food.

Life probably seemed very good to Corbett as he entered the second decade of the twentieth century. Money could be made by working on a logging crew or at a camp for turpentine. There were cattle to chase and hogs to kill. Deer and turkeys could be found in places distant from the settlements, and squirrels made a tasty stew. To judge from Corbett's later life, he, like the animals he hunted, might have shifted occupations with the seasons. It must have satisfied the soul in him that reached back to the edges of the European ice.

The trouble with the history they taught us in public school was that it seldom told me anything I wanted to know. The names of politicians and the dates of proclamations they made and the wars they set off filled the pages of the books. I guess our teacher didn't find it interesting either, for he spent most classes leaning back in his swivel chair and looking out the window while we read to ourselves.

One thing that intrigued me in those days was the absence of bears, deer, turkeys, and wolves in our woods. Corbett claimed they once had been common. Nothing in our school library shed any light on the problem, and later, when I went away to college, even the tons of history books there had nothing to say about it. It was as if politicians and historians had conspired to have the information deleted to give the impression that nothing in history mattered except people and the things they built.

Finally, one year I made a trip to Washington, D.C., and found what I had been looking for. Someone had filed it in the archives of a building labeled the Smithsonian Institution. Here the librarian took me into a back room with no one in it. She pulled from the shelf a couple of cardboard boxes filled with notebook pages written in longhand.

"U.S. Biological Survey" said the labels on the boxes. Wm. L. Bray, Jas. H. Gant, N. Hollister, and Harry C. Oberholser had signed their names to the tops of various pages. I recognized the town and county names that appeared beside the signatures. The dates corresponded to the time of Corbett's youth — 1899, 1902, 1905.

Yes, Jasper County had been different then. Said Oberholser: turkeys frequent the woods and clearings and are tolerably common. Deer are common at Jasper, living in the pine forest. The timber wolf is said to have been common in former years but is now rare. Bears are now not found, except very sparingly; a few are said still to inhabit the "Big Thicket."

Indeed the Big Thicket, fifty miles south of Jasper near Sour Lake, provided the last and best stronghold against hunting. James Gant talked about its animals: turkeys are still common in the "Big Brush" and other thickets near Sour Lake. Deer are numerous all over the Big Thicket but hard to find without dogs or by fire (night) hunting. Wolves are numerous in the thicket and do considerable damage to calves and pigs. They are very sharp and hard to trap or poison. Bears still abound in considerable numbers in the most dense parts of the thicket but are gradually being killed out.

Corbett's stories gained a new dimension. He had helped his neighbor and relative, Red Childers, trap wolves, he had said, some of the last ones. "Uncle" Red had been paid by the government to trap wolves; Granddaddy had trapped them to protect his hogs. He had never talked of hunting bears; others had likely killed them off in his neck of the woods by the time he carried a gun.

"The last turkey I killed," he told me once, "flew up high into a sweetgum a hundred yards or more away. I shot him twice with that little .22 Special before he fell; you could cover the two bullet holes with your hand. I tied his feet to the saddle horn, and his head reached nearly to the ground."

Frontier. Soon after Corbett's youth it would retreat to the recollections of old folks and to notes stored in old museums. Finally, the recollections would die, and eventually even the measure of truth conveyed on paper would be hard to find. Virtual reality would take their place, available in video stores and featuring slit-eyed men with six-guns and big hats against a simple backdrop of horse, cow, and false-front town. Unpeopled woods full of secret places and big, wild animals would be as if they never had existed, except in our imaginations.

11 John Henry and the Iron Horse

Once I built a railroad, now it's done.
Brother, can you spare a dime?
E. Y. Harburg, "Brother, Can You Spare a Dime?"

Abandoned roadbeds the grown-ups called trams stretched through the woodlands of my youth. We followed them like safety lines to help us venture into unknown places. On the flatter ground they made little dent upon the land, and you had to pay attention or you would lose them, but in steeper country you could follow them more easily — they cut gashes across hilltops, made thin benches along hillsides, and rode berms into ravines.

The trams once had carried steam-driven logging trains on rails. People cutting timber in the early twentieth century had pushed into the woods on the trains in a single glorious raid on trees. Then they had retreated, taking with them trains, rails, and furious activity and leaving straight and quiet travelways through younger stands of timber.

A tram ran past our house. Massive beeches, oaks, maples, and hickories shaded it; the loggers responsible for building it had taken even bigger trees, I suppose, half a century before I used it as a trail.

The tramway shot across our fifty acres, into the adjacent tract of forest owned by Corbett's brother, Ragan, and across a swale before climbing up into Ragan's twenty-acre field on the hill beyond. Once I dug into a mound of leaves between the ends of the earthen levees that jutted toward each other across the swale and uncovered remnants of the timbers that had bridged the gap.

In the late 1940s Daddy had made that final corn-growing venture in Ragan's field. He had built a road between our place and Ragan's field by clearing off the briars and brush that had crept onto the tramway following the loggers' exit. In the spring and summer he would travel daily back and forth to work the field with horse and plow. In the fall he harvested the corn, and the horse pulled it home in the wagon.

A lot of people in those days used abandoned trams for travel by wagon and auto, calling them tramroads. One particular tramroad slashed from west to east across the southern part of the Angelina countryside I knew. Everybody called it the Old Kirby Main Line Road. We walked and drove along it and used it as a reference line in mental maps of that country.

For me, the Kirby Main Line started at Delaney Spring, where it sliced through our arrowhead place. Though it continued far beyond to the west, no road followed it in that direction, and I had only a vague notion where it went. Eastward, about a mile from the spring, it dropped off to cross Indian Creek. Just before the incline to the creek, in a swale on the left-hand side, a gash of gray showed where Pa and other homesteaders had mined clay to build their fireplace chimneys. The creek water made a perfectly clear pool just above the crossing, and here Jack and I would sometimes ride with Corbett in his pickup, with barrels in the back, to load on water for the cows.

Beyond Indian Creek, the Main Line road went flat and almost straight for the several miles to the highway that led north out of Jasper. A mile or two short of that so-called North Highway, an abandoned road turned left off the Main Line, climbed a hill, and ended in an open flat where two towering cedar trees marked the place where once a house had stood.

"William Hiram Truett, your great-great-grandfather on your daddy's side, lived here," my mother said on our first visit there. The things that impressed me most about the Hi Truett place were the sharp drop of land at the north end of the old field and the vista beyond. It made my heart thump when I walked up to the brink. It set me to thinking about what a mountaintop might be like.

"Here's the best kind of spot to call a turkey," Corbett once said as we stood there looking out to the horizon, not a house, road, or any other man-made sign to interrupt the view. "In April on a still morning you would be sure to hear them gobblin'."

Of course, he referred to earlier days. Times when there had been wild turkeys.

Like Hiram and his descendants, all the other homesteaders in the land between Delaney Spring and Jasper's North Highway had long since left the sandy countryside for more settled places by the time I traveled the Kirby roadbed. Pa Graham's place had been the last one abandoned, and he, Corbett, and Fannie moved from there in the early 1950s. That left a wonderfully vacant country along the Old Kirby Main Line Road and north all the way to the Angelina River.

Only much later did I learn the story of the man responsible for that long, straight roadway through the pinewoods. He had been well known to generations before me, but somehow the story had ended there. I found him in a book. His name was Mr. John Henry Kirby.

Ten years prior to the time Isaac Nelson Graham had brought his family down the Beef Trail to De Zavala, the Kirby family had made its entry into Texas. They had come on the very same road, said the book, and, like the Grahams, had come from Mississippi.

John Thomas Kirby snapped his whip. The oxen leaned against the yoke and heaved the wagon forward. It rumbled as its wheels hit the planking of the boat. Sarah hiked her dress and stepped aboard with James at six years close in tow; the boy sprang onto the Neches River ferryboat like a rabbit.

Jordan's Ferry, people called it. Soon the Kirbys bumped into the west bank of the Neches. They had come into the Promised Land. Sarah stepped ashore.

John Thomas Kirby found the land he sought twenty-five miles farther down the road at a place called Peachtree Village. The pine trees on the hills towered skyward, sighing in the wind the same as in Mississippi. The hardwoods held a mystic silence in the summer bottomlands at noon. The woods around them seemed no different from the place they'd left behind. Their neighbors, newly come and Bible-toting Anglos like themselves, made this Tyler County settlement a home.

On November 16, 1860, ten days after the American people elected Abraham Lincoln to the presidency of the United States, Sarah bore a second son. This baby first saw daylight in a one-room cabin near the banks of Caney Creek, one of many so-named streams in this land where switch cane flourished in the bottoms. They called him John Henry.

The Civil War soon erupted, and with it came the waste of lives and energies that wars have always brought. Sarah did the best she could to watch the farm and tend the children, but when the elder John came home at fighting's end, he found the fields grown up to weeds and all the cattle gone. John Henry soon turned six.

The war had interrupted an economic lifeway in the South that had been building for many years. Fields that had seen sugarcane and cotton grown by slaves and shipped to distant ports turned to weeds and bobwhite quail. River cities that before the war had prospered from the farm and lumber trade gasped for air. The wealthy planters took the greatest plunge, for they had built their empires on the dual subsidies of captive human labor and money from the outside.

John Thomas and his backwoods neighbors felt the hard times, too, but they bounced back. Like the frontier kindred they had left behind along the roads across the South, few had slaves and most lived hand-to-mouth, growing what they ate and building with materials at hand.

John Henry Kirby later wrote of how his family and their neighbors survived those troubled times:

> During the War between the States, and for eight or nine years afterward, the wife and daughters in each family spun the cloth out of which the family clothing was made. In every home there were two or more spinning wheels, according to the family need, and in the homes of the more fortunate families there was a loom for weaving the cloth . . . of cotton or wool.
>
> In the backyard at each home there was a rope works for the manufacture of plow lines, stake ropes, calf ropes, twine and other such things as needed on the farm. . . .
>
> There were many crude blacksmith shops in every neighbor-

hood and also many woodworking establishments for the manufacture of these vehicles [buggies, buckboards, surreys, and wagons] as well as plows, spinning wheels, looms, and other farm necessities, usually constructed of . . . hickory, ash, white oak, or dogwood.

Turning plows in general use were known as "the Cary plows" and were constructed entirely of wood. . . . Every farmer made his own ox yokes, ox bows, axe handles, hoe handles — in fact all kinds of handles were made of hickory.

Every neighborhood had a sufficient number of cotton gins and cotton presses. Both the gins and the presses were drawn by horses. They were constructed entirely of wood.

In the early years, all of the Piney Woods country had much wild game. Deer, bear, turkey, and squirrel supplied meat for the family table.

All of these counties had some prairie on which could be found large herds of unbranded horses and cattle. . . . There were also domestic hogs gone wild in the creek and river bottoms.

Like most Texas backwoods people at the time, the Peachtree Village folks were primarily self-sufficient, getting by with little help from outside. Being self-sustaining kindled love of freedom. John Henry Kirby grew to manhood in a place where independence grew as naturally as the bounty of the land about him.

In John Henry's teenage years, the education urged upon him by his mother dampened his enthusiasm for plowing land and chopping wood. He devoured book after book by the light of pine-knot fires. Reading convinced him that a more exciting way to travel down the road of life lay just beyond tradition. In particular, he found himself intrigued with the struggles of that martyr of the North, Abe Lincoln.

At the age of nineteen, Kirby went away to school at Woodville, the seat of Tyler County. Professor Frank Pulaski Crow sent him there. Having taught John Henry at a six-month school near Peachtree Village, he persuaded Kirby's father that eighty dollars for tuition, room, and board for a six-month stay in Woodville would bear fruit. Professor Crow also helped to plant another seed — he alerted Lelia Stewart, daughter of a prominent Woodville family, to John's potential as a husband.

Lelia Stewart's parents disapproved of her interest in John Henry.

Even on the frontier, lineage often counted, and John was a struggling farmer's son. Finally, after John had shown his worth by working as a sheriff's deputy, enrolling at Southwestern University at Georgetown, Texas, and serving in the Texas senate as a calendar clerk, his proposals to Lelia brought a "yes." They married at the Methodist church in Woodville on November 14, 1883.

The wedding party smelled of wealth, as was proper for a leading family giving up its daughter. The bridesmaids numbered eight and wore expensive dresses. The men sported Prince Albert coats and silk hats.

Prophetic of things to come, John Henry led his bride aboard the train on the T.S. Railroad, which had just been built north from the coast to Woodville. They pulled away from town and rode to Galveston to spend their honeymoon.

During his time as calendar clerk in the Texas senate, John Henry often worked for Senator S. Bronson Cooper. One of Cooper's assignments that zeroed Kirby in on his career was to analyze the timber situation of the various states — volume estimates, rates of depletion, and so on. When Kirby saw the numbers, he foresaw the future value of East Texas's timber and started sinking all his money into pinelands.

Under Cooper's tutelage, Kirby passed the Texas bar in 1884. Shortly after that, likewise through the offices of Cooper, he met a group of Boston businessmen interested in the advent of the railroad into Texas's timberlands. His ideas merged with theirs, and the Texas and Louisiana Land and Lumber Company took shape, with Nathaniel D. Silsbee of Boston as president and an authorized capital of $1.4 million. Kirby commenced to buy, sell, and trade timberlands for the corporation.

He quickly stepped into the homes and social circles of the Yankee money changers. Tightfisted merchants all, they expected great returns. Many had accumulated wealth from trading opium. Kirby extended his rounds in Boston and New York, seeking more investment money.

In 1890, having made $300,000 profit in the past three years, John Henry and Lelia and baby daughter, Bess May, moved to Houston. At thirty, he had rocketed to local fame.

Kirby needed transportation. Pines paid little profit where they stood. Most were far from waterways. Lumber must be hauled to where the people wanted wood — Gulf Coast towns, central Texas, and seaport cities everywhere.

In June 1893 Kirby started laying rail north from Beaumont. Transportation was on the way. By 1895, the year of Corbett's birth, Kirby's railroad reached the fifty-mile point, and the town of Kirbyville, twenty miles south of Jasper, grew up there. The railroad marched on, to Jasper, Brookeland, and farther. By the late 1890s it had traveled north a hundred miles from Beaumont. It ran along the higher ground, mostly near the eastern edge of the Neches and the Angelina watersheds.

The upland trees began to bleed away to markets of the world. The value of a tract of timberland shot skyward. Once again, as in the days when sailing ships began to ply the seas in search of scarce commodities, transport opened wide the doors of profit.

Kirby did well in the lumber business because he made efficient use of men and bought the best technology. His employees specialized — each man, from the flatheads cutting trees to the managers of the sawmills, had only one main job to do. The latest styles of steam engines burning wood replaced the horses and the men who had powered older operations. Locomotives, skidders, loaders, and sawmills alike filled the forest with their steamy breath.

He standardized logging operations to expedite management. From main-stem railroads, secondary tramroads extended into forests, and temporary branches ran from these to every stand of timber. Teams of men with crosscut saws and axes felled and trimmed the trees. A man and mule pulled the skidder cable from the railcar up to several hundred yards where the logs lay. The skidder operator engaged the power drum, yanking in the cable with its log. Mechanical loaders picked up logs and stacked them onto railcars.

Kirby's railroad sent its tracks deep into the woods. Towns that Kirby named for friends and family sprang up on the central route: Evadale (after a Jasper schoolteacher), Bessmay (after his daughter), Browndell (after John W. Brown, a Baltimore banker and Kirby investor), and Kirbyville itself. At the logging fronts, the smell of fresh-cut pine filled the woods. The "shh-shh-shh" of crosscut saws, the tapping of the wedges, and the crash of falling trees told the skidder

Mr. Kirby's iron horse. A steam engine of the Sabine and Northern Railroad Company among southeast Texas hardwoods in the early 1900s. Courtesy Jasper County Historical Commission.

operator where to send the cable. The whirling skidder drum brought the logs flying back toward the railcars, ripping ground and crushing brush and trees along the way.

A branch of Kirby's railroad followed portions of the old Beef Trail. Some said he did this purposely to trace the route by which his family had come into Texas. Tramroads began to spread from this branch to reach all the corners of that Angelina country I would later on think of as Corbett's and mine. The roadbed of this branch became the Old Kirby Main Line of my younger days.

Kirby's fame climbed with his fortune. The press made him a hero; he became the symbol of the country boy who had made it. Hopeful mothers named their children after him. He moved at ease among the men in business and politics from Austin to the eastern seaboard. He drank toasts with governors in Texas and presidents in Washington.

He loved to be loved. He passed out money and Bibles to employees at Christmastime. He slapped the shoulders of the workers in his lumber towns and called their children by their names. His homespun humor and philosophy delighted country folk, and they placed him on the throne as Baron of the Pinelands.

Things looked good in 1900. His income escalated. He sold his railroad to his friends in Santa Fe at a handsome profit.

Then the next year a Chicago friend introduced him to a New York entrepreneur named Patrick Calhoun. The Spindletop oil strike at Beaumont had Wall Street buzzing, and Calhoun smelled money. He convinced John Henry to join him and other eastern backers to exploit oil and lumber in Kirby's stomping grounds.

Kirby and Calhoun worked out a promoter's agreement in which they set up a business corporation, Houston Oil Company. John Henry put his brand on Houston Oil by adding a venture he called the Kirby Lumber Company. The men agreed that John Henry was to help Houston Oil acquire the ownership of lands in eastern Texas, which they would then explore for oil and exploit for timber. The Kirby Lumber Company would buy the timber from the Houston Oil Company. It sounded slick, and it was.

Kirby built the master plan for operations. At the time, he controlled some 850,000 acres of East Texas timberlands, well over a thousand square miles. He would sell to Houston Oil the lands he owned outright, as well as more land he planned to buy with offers of stock in the Kirby Lumber Company. Houston Oil would give to Kirby Lumber all the tramroads, sawmills, and other lumbering equipment that existed on new lands it bought. Kirby would meet his obligations to Houston Oil by cutting trees and selling lumber.

As the operation got under way, disagreements came about. Investors in the venture sent a timber expert out, who reported that the trees on some land that Houston Oil had bought from Kirby had been cut beforehand. One timber owner would not sell a major tract of timberland that Kirby counted on to meet the obligations made to Houston Oil. Worst of all, Kirby and Calhoun often operated independently and sometimes at cross purposes.

By 1903 Kirby smelled trouble. Lack of detail in the pact with Calhoun, plus Kirby's inabilities to cut the timber as rapidly as promised, led to litigation. By 1904, after a lengthy legal struggle, the Kirby Lumber Company went into receivership. It owed much to Houston Oil, now headed by Calhoun and the other moneylenders. The Yankee boys had fleeced John Henry good.

Prior to his dealings with Calhoun, Kirby had practiced conservation, leaving at the logging front larger trees for seed. But as often happens when a noble goal gets caught in economic straits, conservation took a backseat when creditors came calling. Giving testimony in a lawsuit in 1917, Kirby wrote of what he did to satisfy the debt to Houston Oil:

> At that time [prior to the 1904 receivership] we were patriotic enough to try to make the forest perpetual, and we had sixty foresters down here from the Forestry Department of the United States putting in plans for operating it. When Judge Burns took charge and the corporations were retired, he said he could not practice any altruism, but had to hew to the letter of the contract, and we have done that since February 1904. In instances we may leave a tree probably twelve inches [in diameter], but if we do leave that tree probably the Houston Oil Company at some time can require us to pay for it.

Logging crews in those days moved through the woods in "fronts," cutting the best, or highest grade, trees and leaving those of lesser worth. Between about 1900 and 1920, the railroads pushed into most parts of the Angelina country. The loggers cut the tallest of the pines, put them on the trains, and hauled them away.

Pa Graham found work in Kirby's logging camps as a filer. At home, he had gained familiarity with that Excalibur of the southern pioneer, the crosscut saw. He owned the necessary files, the gauge for setting the length of the raker teeth, the steel spider for setting the angle of the cutter teeth, and the clamp for anchoring the saw blade to a bench.

Corbett likewise signed on with the logging crews as soon as he was old enough. He learned to file saws, fell trees, and hook the logs to the skidder cable. At a young age, he started earning cash.

"Shortly after I married your mother," commences a favorite story of my father's, "Mr. Graham asked me to help him cut some trees. I was young and strong in those days and took a lot of pride in my ability to work. Mr. Graham was a little man, and I was sure it wouldn't take me long to saw him down."

To saw somebody down was to outlast them. But you had to be fair about it; you couldn't ride the saw, that is, press it hard against the log or tree during your partner's pull stroke. I could usually outlast my brother, partly because he was younger and partly because I knew how to ride the saw just enough to tire him but not enough for him to notice.

"Well," Daddy's story continues, "I couldn't beat Mr. Graham. He sawed me down, tired me completely out. I didn't know he had worked as a flathead in lumber camps."

Once Corbett wanted me to help him fell a tree. He brought the saw, double-bit axe, sledgehammer, and wedges to the base of a large sugar maple behind the garden. I can't remember why he wanted it cut — probably for firewood or to enlarge the pasture. I felt some hesitation, for the tree looked well over two feet in diameter and rose eighty to ninety feet into the air.

"Now, we want it to fall this way," he said, pointing to a small opening between two other trees.

The big maple towered nearly vertically but seemed to lean a bit in the direction opposite from where Corbett wanted it to fall. He made a circuit of it, occasionally running his eye up its height.

When he picked up the saw and indicated we should make a cut about a foot above the ground on the same side of the tree as he planned it to fall, I felt bewildered. Maybe I had heard him wrong. But I asked no questions, and soon we had cut four or five inches into the trunk. At that point, he stopped and removed the saw.

"Hand me that axe," he instructed.

He began chopping several inches above the saw cut, angling the strokes downward. I watched. Each stroke landed precisely in line with the previous one. Soon a notch appeared in the tree trunk, its bottom our saw cut.

"Now, let's see where this tree will fall," he said.

Grasping the axe with one hand, he positioned the double-bladed head parallel with the ground and shoved it top-first into the notch. The handle pointed directly at the opening between the two trees.

"All right," Corbett said. "Now let's cut the other side."

We started this cut an inch or so higher than the first one. Periodically I straightened to rest. Corbett waited patiently. As we sawed past center and came nearer and nearer the notch, I straightened more and more often, looking aloft for some indication of movement. The remaining piece of unsawed trunk looked very thin; what if the tree took a notion to fall backward? Or toward one of us?

Finally, Corbett picked up the steel wedge and tapped it gently with the sledge into our saw cut. The tree trembled.

"Here, let's saw some more," he said, removing me from partial paralysis.

I felt the urge to simply slide the saw back and forth, pretending to cut, but he forced it against the last bit of wood that stood between us and catastrophe. When it seemed that the tree must break off and topple in a direction of its own choosing, Corbett straightened and picked up the sledgehammer again.

Against the wedge, the hammer made a steely "thwack!" Looking skyward, I saw the branches move. Slowly, very slowly, the top began to tilt. "Thwack!"

"Don't get behind it!" Corbett suddenly warned. "It might kick back."

Kick back? Which way was behind? I stood frozen as the tree picked up momentum.

"Back up!" he commanded sharply.

I scuttled backward, tripping on a briar. But by the time the tree split the narrow opening and crashed to the ground, I had regained my footing and retreated sufficiently far to feel safe from kickback or any other kind of trick the tree might pull. It had fallen exactly where he wanted it to.

John Henry Kirby's economic plight in the early twentieth century apparently had little noticeable impact on his logging operations. His Prince of Pines image stayed untarnished, perhaps partly because he threw money around freely: if you act like you are rich, most folks will think you are. Many times he borrowed money so he could spend it on his friends. Another Texas tycoon noted that he knew no one but Kirby who was flat broke on $2,000 a month.

In November 1906 John Henry "married off" his daughter, Bess May. He made a social triumph of the wedding, despite the Yankee stature of the groom — a New York mill owner — and the cost of all the trappings, which must have taxed his meager bank account.

The *Southern Industrial and Lumber Review* for December of that year filled a special supplement with accounts of the occasion. The wedding emptied floral shops in Houston; its musical accompaniment approached "concert dimensions." The roll of bills that paid for Bess May's gown, specially made in Europe, might have choked a horse. The yards of cloth used must have been substantial; she had a "large frame" and "weighed out at 280 pounds," according to Jim Wylie, Kirby's body servant and confidant. John Henry and Lelia's wedding gifts included "a rosewood chest of silver containing eleven hundred pieces."

Merchants use the word "production" to describe the transformation of a tree to lumber. To measure this production, they use board feet, sometimes called simply feet — a piece of lumber one foot wide, one foot long, and one inch thick. Lumber production in all the southern states leaped from one billion feet a year when the Civil War ended in 1865 to over twenty billion feet a year when John Henry stoked the boilers of his mills in 1910 to try to pay his debts.

The 1920s saw John Henry, despite his economic woes, wield a heavy hammer in the sphere of politics. He served presidents Warren Harding, Calvin Coolidge, and Herbert Hoover in ways official and less so; the first Buick owned by Coolidge supposedly came as a gift from Kirby. He sometimes used political connections to ease himself past business obstacles.

In demand as a speaker, he took to comparing events and personalities of his time with biblical happenings. Old Abraham was a rugged frontiersman, like the ones in East Texas, he said. "Had he been with us, he would have built a big log house and enjoyed good company."

Kirby struggled on, managing to stay afloat until the Great Depression set in. Then, on May 19, 1933, he filed a voluntary petition of personal bankruptcy with the federal clerk in Houston. He listed assets at

Turning trees into money. A 1927 timber crew hauls an ancient pine from the longleaf woods near the Kirby lumber town of Blox, northwest of Jasper. This single tree yielded 5,280 board feet of lumber and required fourteen mules to pull it out of the woods. Courtesy Jasper County Historical Commission.

almost $13 million, of which $79.91 was cash on hand and $16.77 money in the bank.

The entire populace of Houston gasped. He explained: "The earnings on my properties declined, interest accumulated, taxes increased, and property values went down. Fair market values for my properties still exceed my debts, but there are no purchasers. Kirby Lumber Company is not affected by this action; only my personal affairs are involved."

Friends fell away. He looked in vain for those who had been there by the thousands when he rode the iron horse to victory. A tiny handful helped him out. He got $15,000 per year permanent salary from Kirby Lumber. This and $5,000 a year from the Kirby Petroleum Company (another of his corporations absorbed by creditors) let him continue to travel where the action was.

After Hoover was defeated, John Henry bitterly fought the policies of Franklin Roosevelt. Kirby said, "The people of the South will not tolerate ideas made by scavengers from garbage cans of Europe.

Men and women of pioneer stock will not accept handouts from government."

The labor unions responded: "This man used the sweat of others to enrich himself. Is that not handout by a different name?"

Kirby stood outraged — in Texas, the principles of the free market ranked beside the Ten Commandments. "If any on my twenty thousand-person payroll is dissatisfied," he had said in 1924 in response to the unions' clamor, "then I am not progressing."

Like the mammoth hunter viewing those feasting on his kills, Kirby saw himself as the benefactor of those drawn to his mills and logging camps. He and they participated as partners in the tree-harvesting business. From all accounts, his flatheads and mill operators reciprocated; despite his disproportionate chunk of the pie, they seldom thought of him as riding the saw.

≈"We lived in Call, about ten miles south of Kirbyville, when I was a kid in the late 1920s," says my father. "Call was one of Kirby's milltowns. My daddy worked there as foreman of the sawmill. I went to school in the lower grades."

The 1929 Jasper County census shows several hundred kids in the Call school. Everybody's father worked for Kirby.

"Every Christmas, Mr. Kirby sent a gift to every kid in town," Daddy reminisces. "Nobody got left out. One year I got a train set. It didn't run on batteries or electricity like the ones today; you had to wind it up with a key. I remember that Christmas just like it was yesterday. The track made a circle, and the train went round and round.

"Everybody lived in company houses, which were all pretty much the same," he continues, "but in our time there we lived in several different ones. It became a saying in the family that every year we moved and Mama had another kid.

"Our flour, sugar, lard, and other staple food came from the company commissary. The commissary offices were located upstairs, above the store, and when you paid for items, they sent the money up on a string and someone lowered the change back on the same string.

"We did have a small garden space," he adds. "I raised peppers and sold them in town for fifty cents a gallon.

"A company doctor worked out of an office by the commissary," he goes on. "Once they brought in a man who'd been stabbed, and I squeezed between people's legs to get a look. He lay on a cot, and someone had put a thing like a corkscrew in the hole made by the knife.

"I guess kids wouldn't get to see those kinds of things nowadays," he laughs.

"One thing I didn't like were the hogs that roamed around town. Each house had an outdoor toilet in back with a rear flap for cleaning it out, and sometimes the hogs would get there before the shitwagon. I hated it when one would follow me to the privy and root up the flap just as I sat down.

"Daddy lost his job around 1930," he concludes. "Maybe the mill shut down because of the depression; I don't know. We moved back to my granddaddy's farm near Jasper, and I started following a middle-buster plow in the cotton field to help bring in money. I had finished the fifth grade, and that was the last of my schooling."

In 1935, as Kirby's age approached fourscore, the U.S. Forest Service compiled statistics for the Neches watershed and surrounding countryside. Eighty-four percent of the total forest acreage had been cut. Only one-sixth remained as old-growth timber.

John Henry Kirby died in 1940 at his Houston mansion, no longer wealthy but safe from creditors in a state where a man's home was his castle. No man dies rich, he himself had said, he can only live richly. At the end, he blamed no one for his misfortunes.

If old Abraham had come along about that time, he might have had to search around a bit to find good pines to build that big log house. But cashing out on a store of trees that had taken sun and rain centuries to build seemed the thing to do in those days. It would remain for future generations checking on their savings to decide if Kirby and his men had in fact dipped into the principal.

12 Fannie

Friends may forget you, but never will I.
Postscript of letter from Fannie Griffin to
Corbett Graham, February 16, 1920

"When Boose and I were dating," my mother says, "Mama would get mad if he brought me home past suppertime."

Boose is my father's nickname. His name shows up as Richard on his driver's license and checkbooks, but I never heard anyone call him that. When my 4-H Club leader in grade school asked me his name and then kept pronouncing it "Booze," I felt obliged to correct him, for Daddy had given up alcohol when I was four.

"One time we came home late, maybe ten o'clock," my mother continues, "and Mama had a fit. She and Daddy thought that kind of behavior scandalous. Daddy told me then that he had never been alone with Mama after dark until the night they got married."

If Corbett and Fannie ever hugged each other, it must have been in private. As far as I could tell, they seldom purposely got close, except when crowding together to lift a hog carcass or to pose for a photograph. It is impossible for me to imagine them ever kissing as passionately as I did when I was younger. But I never doubted they belonged together. With few words they collaborated in living, working as a team, each pulling a share of the load. To me, they would not have been complete unless together.

In that time and among those people, everybody knew the difference between men's work and women's work. Most tasks had been assigned by tradition to one gender or the other. Corbett's brother-in-law, Martin, often helped Corbett and Fannie butcher hogs, and he would crank the sausage grinder with enthusiasm until the funnel-shaped feeder reservoir ran out of meat, at which time the grinding would come to a halt until a woman among the workers thought to fill it.

In retrospect, Corbett and Fannie probably shared a much larger number of activities than most at the time considered proper. Fannie often tagged along with Corbett to feed the range cows or to hunt for hogs. He helped her weed the garden and cut corn. Once I heard the tail end of the gossip after Corbett had taken Fannie along on a fishing camp-out on the river with him and his brother, Ragan, though what the disapproval sprang from I never knew. The kinds of activities I saw them share gave me undue expectations later in life of the pursuits men and women should jointly enjoy.

My mother kept a shoe box stuffed with old documents and letters that Corbett and Fannie had saved. Before their death, these mattered little to me, but afterward they began to assume a great deal more importance. These old pieces of paper helped complete the story I knew. It was like going back to the early chapters of a good book after you've jumped ahead and read the final parts.

The shoe box file showed that Fannie, like Corbett, had come from southern roots. S. F. "Shade" Griffin, Fannie's father, caught the tide moving west from Georgia to Texas shortly past the middle of the nineteenth century. He landed on a hardwood hill in Peachtree community, a hundred miles from tidewater and ten miles east of De Zavala.

S. F.'s first wife, Safronie, wore out and died after bearing six children. At her death, he divided up their common property in a will to the children. He wrote it in a small notebook. The writing shows a flair of confidence; the content indicates that substance might have been the poorer part of that frontier legacy:

Mr. S. F. Griffin.

Mrs. A. S. Griffin.

Gave to ther Children

R. M. Griffin 1 cow	$10
1 horse	$30
his [S. F.'s] teeth filling	$8
1 hog	
seed cane, Goos	
Mary Childers	
Received 1 cow	$10
1 saddle	$12.50
teeth filling	$15
1 hog	
Mary received	$2.50
J. H. Griffin	
Received 1 cow	$10.00
1 horse	$60.00
1 hog	
Shade Griffin [Jr.]	
Received 1 cow	$10.00
1 hog	
1 tceth filling	$20.00

107

Fannie

S. F. and Safronie probably owned a tract of farmland in addition to their hogs and cows and tooth fillings. Most rural families did in that neck of the woods. Perhaps S. F. kcpt their land so he could start over; he was only fifty-two. In any case, land to farm was plentiful. The kids could get their own.

Soon after Safronie's death, S. F. took another wife, Susie Hinson. Susie, like S. F., had been married once before, but there had been no children. She was younger than S. F. by eighteen years. Older women might not have been available and, more important, might have passed the age of bearing children.

Their first child died soon after birth. S. F. and Susie tried again, and they had a blue-eyed girl. This was to be their only child. They named her Fannie Lela, and she came into their household on the Peachtree hammock hilltop in August 1902. Down in Old Zavala by the Angelina River, Corbett Graham had reached seven by this time.

Fannie got her formal education at the Peachtree school and her notion of important things from backwoods farmers. Living on a piece of countryside where the hardwoods had built a modest fertility in the soil, she learned early that to farm was to prosper. The best-dressed of her friends had fathers in the fields from dawn to dusk.

I have a photo taken of the teacher and thirty-two kids at Peachtree school in 1912. The teacher wears a tie. Fannie stands near the center of the front row, looking very serious. Her black hair parts right down the middle and has been pulled severely to the rear; perhaps it's made into a bun behind her head like it was when I was young. She and two girls to her right wear knee-length dresses, dark stockings, and shoes. On either side they're flanked by other girls, all barefoot.

By the time Corbett came to her attention, Fannie may have been less sure about the farming option being the best one for him. By this time he had moved with his family to the northern edge of Peachtree to the Pa Graham place of my youth, two miles away from Fannie's home. Rails had come into the woods, and Fannie had heard that he made good money working in the lumber camps. Fannie knew that, since he was the oldest son in the family, he would bring some of the earnings home to help his older sister, Sadie, and the younger ones. Corbett's family lived along the margin of the piney woods, and Fannie's neighbors said it must be hard for them to grow crops in that sand.

Perhaps Fannie and Corbett met at church. They did not meet at school, for he had finished with what education he got by the time she started school. In any case, by 1919, Fannie's sixteenth year, they had struck up an acquaintance more than passing.

The Griffins got their mail at Jasper, ten miles away from home by horse. In early 1919 Fannie suddenly commenced to take an interest any time a neighbor went to town. Was there mail for her? Oh yes, there was a letter.

*The best-dressed kids wore shoes. Fannie Griffin (front row, fifth from right)
stands beside two other girls with shoes and stockings in this 1912 Peachtree school
photo. Courtesy Mac's Studio, Jasper, Texas.*

Brookeland Texas
April 9/1919

Miss Fannie Griffine

Jasper Texas

How are you by this time? Fine I hope. I am getting along fine ex-
cusing a storm we had last weak it blue trees right and left where I
was, I ges the bad man was after me for telling that story I diden
think I wood stay but one weak but you see how it is, I am at
Brookelan I have abought four days work to do before I come home
so it will be about sunday or monday before I get home, yours
trulley

R. L. Graham

Brookeland lay fifteen miles northeast of Peachtree. More than
fifteen years earlier, it had grown up around the Santa Fe rail line, originally Kirby's railroad. At Remlig, a few miles southeast of Brookeland,
Alexander Gilmer (Remlig spelled backward) had installed a large
sawmill in 1905, which lasted until all available timber in the region
was taken. It closed in 1925. Gilmer's lumber business almost certainly
provided the work Corbett did near Brookeland.

Perhaps Corbett did return home by Monday. Given the season, he might have been needed to plant crops. Neither he nor Fannie left any correspondence for several months thereafter. During this time, Fannie turned seventeen. Their romance must have progressed well, for he wrote her soon after he left again, this time to take a job at a turpentine camp in Louisiana:

Joyce La

November 30/1919

Miss Fannie Griffin

Jasper, Texas

Dear friend,

How are you by this time fine I hope, I had a fine trip over here, it was raining when I left Jasper and was still raining when I arrived. I am at Ringwood a turpentine camp about sixty miles East of Axalander [Alexandria], L.A. I got a notice from Pete [one of Corbett's brothers] to com at once I left home thursday and arrived friday night we have plenty of good water to drink. A good place to work Pete and me is going to bild a side camp in a few days.

One of us is coming home Christmas I dont know witch it will be. I am pretty sure it will be Pete I think it will be abought sixty days before I come home that will be as long as I can work over here. Say girl go to the singing convachion and have a good time for me, tell my girl helo for me, that is if you see her. I will clos sending you my adress yours. truly

R. L. Graham

Joyce, L.a.

in care Western Naval Store Co.

Turpentine and rosin distilled from pine gum had been used for many years to waterproof and maintain wooden ships. World War I stimulated a great demand for these so-called naval stores, for ships of steel had yet to make ones of wood obsolete. Though the war ended in late 1918, demand for naval stores for other uses such as turpentine solvent continued; the following year saw the all-time peak of naval stores produced in Texas.

Old-growth longleaf produced the best gum. Western Naval Stores Company, the major operator in western parts of the South, located

110

Fannie

the best virgin stands ahead of the logging fronts and set up camps. Turpentiners cut faces on the sides of large pine trees and fitted galvanized iron gutters and a cup below each face to collect the gum that leaked out.

Corbett may have worked in turpentine camps prior to 1919. The town of Turpentine sprouted in 1907 in the piney woods twenty miles northwest of Jasper. This central camp for the Western Naval Stores Company closed soon after the war ended, to the great relief of many local mothers, who considered turpentiners a rowdy and lawless lot.

> Jasper, Texas,
> Dec. 11, 1919

Mr. R. L. Graham,
Dear Friend,

I sure was glad to hear from you and to hear you were well this leaves me well and I hope it will find you the same.

I am in town to day, I went to the post office [a] while ago and got your letter. I am glad you have a good place to work, and good water. I hope you have lots good to eat & a good bed. "Oh Yes" I didn't get to go to the convention, or see your girl either. . . . I looked for you the other day till there wasn't any fun in looking, and haven't seen you yet two mo. seems like a mighty long time to me and you so far away. I thought I would get to see you Ixmas anyhow. Now don't let what I say bother you, for I may say anything. Well you may excues bad writing and all mistakes as there is too much noise to write.

Hoping to hear from you very soon and a long letter. I remain yours as ever,

> Fannie Griffin

111
Fannie

Corbett must have come home for Christmas, for the next letter from Fannie, dated January 8, 1920, complained: "Corbett I haven't heard a word from you since I did see you." But also: "That sure was a nice [Christmas] present, and a very much appreciated one from you."

Two more letters from Corbett in quick succession smoothed Fannie's feathers. News of floods and mud filled most of the letters; rain had not stopped by late January.

Miss Fannie Griffin

Jasper Texas

Dear friend

How are you getting allong this bad day very well I ges, it is poring down rain over here now say girl the wolfs howled all night last
night they are over here by the hundreds, you can ges what kind of a
place this is, well I here the bell I had beter go and get a bit to eat.

helo I have got back from dinner and my ink has all turned to a
carpenter pencil these lofesters [loafers?] has used it all up while I
was filing up all the handsaws, say I think its coming a flud over here
it is still poring down rain ha-ha we are going to have a party over
here tomorrow night I have found me a sweet heart over here she
has got black hire [hair] keen black eyes, she is a pretty fancy little
girl. . . . dont let my chickens all dround, and how is pigie getting
along fine I ges Well I had beter close for this time so by by yours
trulley

R. L. Graham

The country around the Louisiana turpentine camp of Ringwood
must have been thinly settled; people in similar country in East Texas
had eliminated most "wolfs" by this time.

Jasper, Texas

Feb. 2, 1920

Mr. R. L. Graham

My dear Friend,

I received your letter of Jan. 23 this evening. I sure was glad [to
hear] from you, I sure have been keeping up a racket because I
couldn't hear from you. I guess you are mad at me for not writing
sooner, but I have not had any chance to mail any letter till Sat. and
I wouldn't send one then. I thought you would be home.

You can stay with that black eyed girl just as long as you please.
"But remember" what we saw at the Reunion,

You said you all were going to have a party, I guess you had a
good time, hope so any way. I got an invitation to a party the day you
left over here. I did not go. I have not been anywhere since I went to
the Ixmas tree.

As for your chickens I don't know anything about them but my chickens and pig are alright I guess, they are just as much trouble as ever.

We sure are having some pretty weather now.

Well I guess I had better close as it is getting almost bed time I think. This leaves me well and I hope it will find you the same. Remember me as the little blue eyed girl who thinks just as much of you as ever.

Good night, happy dreams

I remain as ever Yours,

Fannie Griffin

Corbett wrote again on February 11. But five days later Fannie had not yet received the letter. She thought and thought about his last letter and remembered what her friends had said about those turpentine camps. She wrote Corbett again.

Jasper, Texas
Feb. 16, 1920

Mr. R. L. Graham

Mr dear Friend,

I will write you once again. I wrote you about the first of Feb. but I don't know whether the letter reached the post office or not So I will try again.

Corbett the last letter I got from you was wrote the 23rd of Jan. which has been over three weeks.

You told me the last time I saw you that you were coming home the last of Jan. This is the middle of Feb. Three Sundays I have spend looking for you and I have not seen you yet. Have you decided to stay over there and work? It looks to me like it is time everybody that intends to farm were at work in the fields. If you don't intend to farm, go ahead. I don't suppose you think it is any of my business what you do. And I have about decided that too.

Go ahead with the other girl if you think more of her than you do of me, she is the one for you. . . .

Well I hope this will find you well. I am just fine I guess I weighed 143 last Sat.

I had beter close and get to cooking supper.

I hope you will take time to answer my letter and tell me what you figure on doing if you don't object to my knowing. hoping to hear from you real soon.

I remain yours,

Bye, Bye
Fannie

Leaves may wither, flowers may die
Friends may forget you, but never will I

Corbett may have worried a bit about this letter. But he now worked as a carpenter at the camp and made good money. He enlisted his mother's support to put off coming home to begin spring plowing.

Joyce La
Feb, 29/1920

Miss Fannie Griffin
Deare Friend

I ges you are lookin for me to day it look like I wont never get to come home. I thought I wood get to see you to night, I call up Mama this morning over the telephone she said I cud stay to more weaks I am only getting seven dollars and seventy ¢ a day

I worked whin I first cam over here but I am not working now I am working the other fellow having a easy time I had beter close for this time I got a litter from you friday I will rite agan abought tusday if nothen goes rong I will see you second sunday night so by by

R. L. Graham

By mid-March Fannie seemed a little worn from waiting: "You said . . . you would be home in two weeks, I looked and wondered. . . . I am tired tonight as I have been cutting some of them awful briars. . . ."

Corbett must have worried a little more by this time. Spring had come, and you never could tell what a woman might do once the smell of flowers filled the air. He dashed off another letter.

Joyce La
March, 15/1920

Miss Fannie Griffin
Dear friend

How are you getting along fine I ges, all except worid and mad say girl every time I get a letter from home som body has ran away

and married there is four that I know I dont know what coses it unless it is leapyear, I ges that is the reson. I ges you will [be] gon when
I get home I will be at hom befor leapyear is gon I ges it dont look
like it

  If I keep getting plenty of dear to eat I will get fat I don't weight
but 157 lbs that is the most I every weighed in my life, you wont
know me whin I get home I have mended so much well I had better
close I will see you some sweet day by and by   R. L. Graham

Perhaps Corbett sang to himself as he sawed and hammered. People
made up a lot of work songs in those days.

I've been workin' all in the rain
Tied to a dirty old ball and chain,
O dear Fannie, I'll come home some sweet day . . .

Turpentiners were not the only rural people to live off "dear" in the
spring. Before long, though, people everywhere in these rural areas
would have eaten up all the deer and would turn to hogs.

  Soon Corbett came home to farm. On August 13 Fannie had her
eighteenth birthday. Two weeks later, after all the beans had been
canned and the corn laid by, she and Corbett married. He had saved a
thousand dollars, and with it they bought a hundred-acre farm and a
house on the other side of the Angelina River at a place called Plum
Ridge.

As Corbett seemed pleased to report to Fannie, he earned nearly
eight dollars per day as a laborer in the lumber camps. This had
seemed a modest wage to me until I calculated that 130 days of work
had bought their farm outright. In terms of real value, his wage had
been substantial — at twenty-five and working part-time, he had captured what many today at twice that age only dream about.

  To get a better picture of where Corbett's money had come from, I
searched around for documents about those early days of the timber
industry. The best one I located had been written in 1935 by two federal foresters named J. W. Cruikshank and I. F. Eldredge. These men
described the forests Kirby and other lumbermen had sold to get the
money to pay Corbett and other workers. They described the forests
in the early 1900s, before Kirby's railroads reached them.

Uncut old-growth pine stands generally are stocked with 20 to 50 mature trees per acre, containing 4,000 to 15,000 board feet. Under-growth is seldom present.... The old growth timber stands are characterized by trees varying in age from 70 to over 150 years.

The hardwood group consists of the upland-hardwood, bottom-land-hardwood, scrub-hardwood, and cypress-tupelo types.... Most important [in acreage] is the bottomland-hardwood type.... It occurs along the Sabine, Neches, Trinity, and smaller rivers. Red and black gum, red and white oaks, magnolia, ash, and cypress are commonly found in these bottoms....

The upland-hardwood type is composed of mixed hardwoods, such as post oak, southern red oak, black oak, red [sweetgum] and black gum, and hickory. This type occurs in small areas scattered throughout [Southeast Texas].... The scrub-hardwood type is a mixture of stunted, low-quality hardwoods of little commercial value, occurring where soil or moisture conditions do not favor rapid tree growth.

By 1935 84 percent of the Southeast Texas woods had been logged. The timber barons had clear-cut the best longleaf stands.

Only three percent of the forest area, or slightly over 200,000 acres, is clear-cut. Practically all of this [clear-cut acreage] is found in areas originally stocked with longleaf pine. Extensive acreages [of clear-cut pinelands] occur northwest of Jasper in the rolling up-lands bordering the Neches and Angelina rivers....

The best hardwoods had been cut as well.

Young trees of varying sizes and ages are intermingled with the older merchantable trees, and when the latter are logged, necessarily by a rough selection system [instead of by clear-cutting], there is always sufficient advance growth remaining to provide for the continuance of well-stocked stands. Openings provided by removal of the mature trees are soon [naturally] restocked with seedlings. Since, however, the common practice is to remove the best trees and especially the more valuable species, the hardwood types must eventually deteriorate in commercial value....

*High-grading the hardwoods. This crew south of Jasper about 1900 is cutting oak
staves for making wooden barrels. Like everyone else, they took the best trees first.
Courtesy Jasper County Historical Commission.*

The deterioration in commercial value of the timber since Corbett's
day didn't seem entirely to explain why the modern timber company
employee can't pay for a house at twenty-five. I needed to know more.

By now I had lost some confidence in the TV economists, so I went
to the economics section of the library. There I found the most con-
spicuous volumes to be even less interesting than ordinary history
books. But occasionally among them I located thin books I could understand. Some of these even used sensible logic.

I found a term I had heard Corbett use — high-grading. To high-
grade is to selectively take the best, said the thin books, like the loggers
had done in Corbett's youth.

Under a free market system, the books explained, high-grading
typifies not only logging but the use of all resources — farming, pumping oil or water, all kinds of mining. It makes economic sense in a competitive market, because more money can be made where extraction is
cheaper. But it also ensures that each succeeding generation of users
will need to work harder to extract an equivalent amount of wealth

from the land. Over time, it depletes the productivity of landscapes and nations.

I had never heard the TV economists express worry about that. No problem, they said. If we run out of something, we'll always find something else to use as a substitute. We always have.

It seemed very complicated, and I wasn't sure whom to believe. Maybe the question of whether Corbett and Fannie had been wealthier than me would clear up later.

13 Mr. Ford's Car

Born of the sun they traveled a short while toward the sun,
And left the vivid air signed with their honor.

Stephen Spender, "I think continually of those who were truly great"

If in 1920 Corbett could have looked ahead, he would have seen his daily life shaped more and more by men in other places. Those distant people brought control by temptation, not by force. They offered more convenient ways of doing work that had been done before by human sweat.

By harnessing new energies and fashioning new gadgets, industrialists would bring John Henry Kirby's dream to many. Everyone could have an iron horse, but only if they sacrificed a measure of the freedom that had up to then let them carry on their lives independently of bosses.

An event that forewarned of change had taken place sixty miles downstream from Old Zavala in 1901. On January 10 of that year, the town of Beaumont awoke to the sounds of the same saws that had made it sleep the night before. Trains on Kirby's railroad rolled in from the north. Millhands started work at shaping boards from timber.

Dockhands at the Neches River landing loaded wood on steamers bound for distant ports.

The time approached mid-morning. Some had paused for coffee. At 10:30 by the railroad stationmaster's watch, a low-pitched roar commenced from somewhere to the south. Those who heard it paused to listen, then to look.

"It's Bud's well!" someone shouted.

Three miles outside town at a low hill on the marshy plain, no one had to shout. Patillo "Bud" Higgins's wooden derrick had transformed itself. With the roar, three hundred feet of drilling pipe shot skyward through the structure. Inky liquid spouted up a hundred feet. Spindletop had come to life, and the Age of Oil had begun.

≈≈Hardly anyone in those days suspected oil had come originally from sunshine. It all started millions of years ago near the edges of tropical oceans. Here, sunlight on the water stimulated tiny plants, called plankton, to grow. These kinds of plants are what make ponds fertilized by cattle droppings green in summer.

Year after year in that faraway time, rain on land brought loads of silt, clay, and life-nourishing nutrients to the edge of the sea. A plankton soup simmered in the bays and estuaries. A drizzle of mud and plankton settled in the coastal waters, collecting on the bottom with dead invertebrates and fish. Century after century the dead plants and animals built up, layer on layer. Bacteria decomposed them, leaving behind in the bottom ooze oil and a gas called methane.

Thousands of years passed, and the delta of a great river built seaward to form land where Beaumont now stands. The river shifted its point of discharge many times as its delta moved back and forth across the shallow sea. Silty mud settled where the water smoothed and stilled; sand layered deep in turbulent places.

The mud and sand weighed down on deeper layers. The grains of sediment pressed closer and closer against each other. Gradually the great pressure forced the oil and gas left by the decomposition of the plankton out of the layers of mud and clay and into nearby layers of sand which had larger spaces between the grains.

The pressure eventually became so great that both the mud layers and the sand layers hardened into rock. The mud became shale or mudstone, impervious to oil or gas; the sand turned to porous sandstone, and in the pores the oil and gas collected.

The oil and gas seeped upward in the sandstone until they ran into a layer of shale. There they stopped. In some places, ancient movements of the earth's crust had tilted the shale layer, and the oil and gas oozed uphill along its bottom. Where the tilt leveled out, then dipped again, the oil and gas stopped, trapped beneath a cap of shale.

For many millions of years the sediments kept building up at the surface; pressures became greater and greater where the ancient seabed had been, squeezing out even more oil and gas from the sediments. The store of oil and gas grew and grew.

Then one day Bud Higgins's drillers pierced the cap of shale at eleven hundred feet below the ground, and the pressure from the gas sent drilling pipe and oil sky-high. A stock of fuel built by a hundred million years of sunshine on the sea shot heavenward, as if reaching for its origins. The energy that would change the course of Corbett's life spilled out on the ground.

More than forty years before Bud Higgins's drilling crew made the strike at Spindletop, Edwin Drake had drilled a well for oil in Pennsylvania. They sold Drake's find as "mineral oil"; people used it to lubricate, to light, and to heat. The size of Higgins's discovery — eight times as much as any previous well — spurred quests for better ways to use oil.

The ancient Greeks attributed visionary foresight to Prometheus, the mythical Titan who stole fire from heaven and imparted it to mortals. A Promethean zeal took hold of engineers when they began to understand the vastness of the oil deposits; each strove frantically to be the first to put the fire contained therein at work to serve mankind. Maybe some of them envisioned mythic hero status.

Inventors by the early twentieth century had arranged a trial marriage between a by-product of oil and an engine. The by-product they called gasoline. They named the type of engine, conceived in principle two hundred years before, internal combustion.

Before the twentieth century opened, engineers in Europe and

America were testing ways to hook these engines onto wagon wheels to carry people over land. Hiram Percy Maxim, son of a firearms inventor, found himself among the troops that led the charge to build a horseless carriage. In his later years he wrote: "As I look back, I am amazed that so many of us began work so nearly at the same time. . . . In 1892, when I began my work on a mechanical road vehicle, I suppose there were fifty persons in the United States working on the same idea. . . ."

Maxim's enthusiasm for using internal combustion germinated when he dropped a lighted match into a cartridge case filled with vaporized gasoline and air. "It was evident," he wrote, "that there was about a thousand times more kick in a drop of gasoline than I had pictured in my wildest flights of imagination."

≈One summer morning in 1876, an Irish immigrant living near Dearborn, Michigan, arose before daylight and hitched his horses to the wagon. His wife had died soon after childbirth a few months before. When the team was ready, he called his thirteen-year-old son; they climbed aboard and set out for nearby Detroit.

The boy still showed signs of grieving for his mother. Indeed, his memory of her and the lessons she had taught would drive him throughout life. Your duty will be hard, disagreeable, and at times painful, she had said. But you must do it.

Several hours on their way, an extraordinary sight hove into view. Huffing and rattling down the road came a wagon without horses. As they drew abreast, the young teenager bounded down to get a closer look. Steam engines that were used to power farm machinery had become a common sight on horse-drawn wagons, but what had caught the youngster's eye was the chain that ran from the engine to the wagon's axle and propelled the entire load.

The boy assaulted the driver with a string of questions. Who made this power unit? How many turns a minute did this engine run?

Then he climbed back onto his father's wagon, and they continued their ride to Detroit. The youngster's name was Henry Ford.

Three years later Henry ran away from home to find a job in Detroit. The oldest major settlement on the shores of the Great Lakes, this city had built itself on transportation. It reigned as the capital of commerce on the New World's greatest inland sea. The region's timber, coal, and copper and iron ores went away by water; goods from elsewhere came by water.

Right away, Ford took an apprenticeship at the James Flower and Brothers Machine Shop. Shortly thereafter, he moved to a job with Detroit Dry Dock Company, pioneers of iron ships and steel manufacture. After that, he worked for the Westinghouse Company in southern Michigan, servicing steam engines Westinghouse had sold to farmers. Then in 1891 he graduated to a four-year stint supervising the steam generators at the Edison Illuminating Company in Detroit — the electrical industry had blossomed after Thomas Edison had invented the incandescent light just over a decade earlier.

The experience Ford gained at these jobs soon set him to experimenting with the dream he had nurtured since that day he saw the horseless carriage on the road to Detroit. In 1888 he had taken his first look at the latest rage of the mechanical world, an internal combustion engine. On display in Detroit, it had been dubbed the Silent Otto for one of its German developers, Nikolaus August Otto. Henry saw how remarkably light and compact it was in comparison with steam engines, and he viewed it as the key to fulfilling his dream.

Eight years later, after he and his friends had planned and tinkered for endless nights in a machine shop at Edison Illuminating Company, Ford finished his first car. The light five hundred–pound vehicle was the second one to appear on the streets of Detroit; the first, a heavy one brought forth by Charles King a month earlier, had chugged along at five miles per hour. Ford's car put this in the shade with an astounding speed of over twenty miles per hour.

But as Ford was to find throughout his life, intense focus on one thing led to neglect of others. He and his colleagues had assembled the car inside a building with only a standard-sized door. They had to demolish several courses of brick in the wall to get it out.

Over the next decade, Ford experimented with improvements. He found financiers eager to invest money in his work, for many saw potential profits to be made. With help from various engineers, he built racing cars to whet the public's interest and to energize himself.

He began to crystallize a dream to build a car for common people. Others by this time also manufactured cars — Oldsmobile, Cadillac, Buick, Packard — but only wealthy people could afford to buy and maintain them. Many sleepless nights he worked.

Each new model seemed to bring him closer to his dream. He built models A through K, except that D and F never materialized. Models R and S took shape. He moved the engine cylinders from horizontal to vertical. He began to cast them as a single block rather than as separate units. French builders brought to his attention lighter, stronger alloys of steel.

Then in 1908, three months after his forty-fifth birthday, he unveiled the Model T. It contained the basic engine configuration that was to persist in autos through the twentieth century. Ford had designed it specifically to meet the needs of working-class Americans — it was light, strong, simple, and inexpensive compared with other cars of the day. It went on the market in October 1908 at $825 and, within a year, more than ten thousand had been sold.

Ford decided to keep the Model T design for the foreseeable future and to concentrate on quantity. Production and sales rose astronomically in the ensuing years, often doubling from one year to the next. In 1913 he introduced a novel idea into his River Rouge plant in Detroit — the moving assembly line. This not only gave birth to a great leap in productivity, it also showed Ford the advantages of uniformity — in automobile parts, in factory operations, and in workers.

As Ford's fame and fortune accelerated, so did his desire to control his entire operation. He purchased iron and coal mines near the Great Lakes for steel production and Brazilian rubber tree plantations for tires. He bought vast timberlands, for in those days wood comprised much of the body of the car. He bought a fleet of ships to bring the materials to the River Rouge plant and to ship the automobiles to dealers throughout the world.

By the early 1920s people everywhere knew the Ford Motor Company as the greatest industrial enterprise in the world. Model T cars rolled off the assembly line at almost four a minute, and city laborers and farmers alike waited in line to buy them. Ford and his flivver — slang at the time for cheap car — embodied the commencement of a second industrial revolution, one fueled by oil.

Through experience, Ford decided that efficient productivity depended on strict control of workers. Though he sometimes paid his employees well, he, like John Kirby, fought with the labor unions to minimize their interference with his operations. He found it increasingly difficult to tolerate displays of independence or individuality in those around him. A great business is too big to be human, he proclaimed.

Aldous Huxley in 1932 envisioned a Brave New World of the future in which people measured time in years since the death of a past messiah named Ford. Babies were conceived and nurtured in test tubes, and schools that were run like assembly lines conditioned individuals to perform specific tasks and to fit predestined social roles. Machines provided shelter, stimulus, and instruction. Periodic religious services began with the First Solidarity Hymn:

> Ford, we are twelve; oh, make us one,
> Like drops within the Social River;
> Oh, make us now together run
> As swiftly as thy shining Flivver.

By the time the last Model T rolled off the assembly line in 1927, fifteen million had been sold to people hungry to move at a faster pace. Drivers and passengers became like the projectiles of their ancestors. Perhaps, as with spears and bullets, speed symbolized power. Whatever the case, Ford's car seemed irresistible.

In 1921, the year following their marriage, Corbett and Fannie moved from the home of Fannie's parents in Peachtree to the hundred-acre farm at Plum Ridge. Though only about ten miles directly northwest of Peachtree, Plum Ridge seemed to Fannie a different world. It lay on the west side of the Angelina River in southern Angelina County, very near the Jasper County line.

The dozen or so families already at Plum Ridge had selected the site with an eye to living off the land. The homesteads perched upon a series of benches that extended from the bases of longleaf pine sandhills to overlook the Angelina River floodplain. Behind the settlement, grass for grazing cloaked the hills of the open pinelands; in front, fertile bottom with its hardwoods and game stretched two miles to the river; in between, on the flatness of the benches, fields and houses stood safe from flooding.

On a topographic map, the Plum Ridge benches show up as peninsulas of equal elevation, projecting like the fingers of a hand from the hills into the river bottom. The benches lie a hundred feet or so above the floodplain. Each projection offers several tens of acres flat enough

Fannie loved that place. Here at Plum Ridge in early winter 1924, she holds daughter Versie. The river terrace fields lie fallow and, beyond the screen of trees, the flatland falls away to the Angelina bottom.

to farm. Between the flats flow clear, tiny streams, originating in the hills as pinewoods springs.

The Graham farm occupied a portion of one bench, some sloping land that crossed a creek, and a piece of Angelina River bottomland. The house and sheds stood at the northern edge of the bench and overlooked the creek and the river bottom. A wagon road ran beside the house, sloping northward to the creek and running southward arrow-straight across the bench through Corbett's cornfield. The road snaked through the two-mile-long settlement, house to house, running more or less parallel to the river.

The Plum Ridge benches always seemed to me a curiosity among these hills, where land is hardly ever flat except in bottomlands. Corbett and the other Plum Ridge residents may not have wondered how the benches came to be and, even if they had, most likely could have found no one to tell them in those days. If someone can't tell you, look in a book, my father had always advised, and there I found the explanation.

Geologists call the benches terraces. Terraces overlook floodplains from Texas to the eastern seaboard as well as rivers elsewhere in the world. They are remains of ancient river floodplains, laid down in the geologic past when the riverbed was higher. The Plum Ridge benches probably took shape in the latter part of the Ice Ages, before the first human set foot in the Angelina country.

Several circumstances may have prompted Corbett to select this homestead at Plum Ridge. First, his older sister, Sadie, and her husband, Martin, lived nearby. Second, the Kirby timber train had just pushed into these pinelands; two miles away the lumber town of Blox had grown up almost overnight in 1918, offering employment. Third, and perhaps not least, the grassy pinewoods at his back door, unlike the Peachtree hammock in which Fannie's parents lived, made prime cattle country. Most was free for grazing. From all accounts, Corbett found riding horseback to tend cattle more "satisfactory" than plowing fields.

So my grandfather and grandmother settled down to make their living from the land, subsidized a bit by John Henry Kirby. They kept a cow or two around the place for milk. Fannie gathered turnips, collards, and kohlrabi from her winter garden and, when spring came, planted sweet potatoes, black-eyed peas, okra, and squash. Corbett plowed the fields of corn and cotton with Old Queenie, their only horse, and they ate the corn and fed it to their stock. Wild woods hogs provided meat for home consumption; beef they sometimes ate but mostly sold because a carcass often spoiled before two people and their neighbors could consume it. They drew water from the well by hand and heated it in iron pots to wash the clothes. Kerosene, or "coal oil," lamps let them work into the night.

By 1929 they had progressed far by dint of effort and frugality. Their daughter, Versie — my mother — reached six that year. Corbett's herd of cows ranged far into the pinelands, and his woods hogs could be found along the pinewoods creeks, in the nearby Angelina bottoms, and on across the river almost as far away as Peachtree. Corbett had a patch of sugarcane in a low place near the river bottom; he dammed the creek to irrigate the cane. Syrup made from cane saved on buying sugar. For a few years Corbett planted cotton but gave it up when prices dropped.

The chuga! chuga! chuga! of Mr. Ford's auto could be heard occasionally up and down the wagon roads. The Grahams counted up the money they had saved from selling cows and hogs and from Corbett's working on the lumber crews. In the year the Great Depression fell, they took a giant step. They bought a new Model T, still the favorite of American country folk though discontinued at the Detroit plant two years before. No one else in Plum Ridge owned a car.

The Model T expedited commerce for the Grahams. With it they could haul a steer's carcass to the Jasper butcher. Fannie drove the car to Blox and peddled pork, eggs, and butter to the lumber workers, staying until after dark on Saturday to get paid for the things she had sold that week.

Ford vehicles in those days, and indeed all early cars, proved more temperamental than modern ones. The Model T started by a hand-crank lever inserted in front, and you had to be careful not to put your thumb around the crank handle or it could break a hand or arm if the engine backfired. Once Fannie cracked a front tooth when the crank kicked back; the dentist fixed it with a crown of gold that fascinated me when I was young.

Though Ford's car had its weaknesses, almost all Model T owners could maintain their own vehicles. People carried flattened bars of iron to take tires off the rims; they used pieces of rubber to patch punctured tubes. Tires proved to be the biggest maintenance problem; the tubes were always getting holes in them from nails and thorns. With a few simple tools, operators could locate, and usually repair, even major damages.

Although the Model T claimed the prize for simplicity, all cars in those days invited maintenance by the owner. One writer of early automobile manuals advised prospective buyers of secondhand cars that they should first inspect the car: "dismantle engine, and examine condition of cylinders and bearings. If bearings are scored or cylinder manifests any crack when a candle or incandescent light is put inside the cylinder in the dark, the car should not be bought."

Early autos had many uses other than to carry people down the road. In demonstrations to farmers, Henry Ford delighted in jacking up his Model T on one side, removing a wheel, and attaching a power belt to the wheel drum to operate a circular saw or corn husker. At Plum Ridge, Corbett bolted a cast-off motor to a wooden frame to turn the sugarcane crusher that he had operated before with Old Queenie. He made natural-rubber shoes for the family out of worn-out tubes and crowbars from cast-off axles. Old farm cars did not go to wrecking yards; owners recycled them.

When the stock market crashed in October 1929 and brokers and bankers jumped from high-rise office windows, Corbett and Fannie barely noticed. Over the next few years, as the Great Depression deepened, they found it harder to get money, but they simply bought less. Most of their necessities and satisfactions came from the land about them; money could be done without if necessary.

They did keep their Model T. By now it seemed almost a necessity. Kirby's lumber business boomed, and Fannie kept her business down in Blox.

The mid-thirties approached, and two circumstances unrelated directly to the deepening depression made Corbett suddenly uneasy with their location. In 1933 the lumber operation at Blox, having stripped the nearby land of trees, picked itself and its workers up and moved to uncut stands of timber out of daily Model T range. To make things worse, the federal government began buying up cutover land near Plum Ridge to put into a national forest system, and free range for grazing cattle near the Graham homestead seemed about to end.

In 1936 Corbett made two changes. He sold the Plum Ridge place for $750 — $250 less than he had paid in 1920 — and moved the family back to Peachtree onto a piece of hammock land. Second, he sold the Model T for $22.50 — he had wanted $25.00, but the buyer somehow already owned one of the wheels, so Corbett knocked $2.50 off the price.

Fannie had not wanted to leave Plum Ridge, but the move to Peachtree gave them some advantages. The hammock soil grew better crops than the Plum Ridge terrace land, which had been the only flood-free zone at Plum Ridge fit for growing anything. Corbett already ran hogs on the timber company land between Peachtree and the Angelina River to the north, and free grazing seemed likely to last longer there than at Plum Ridge. Despite the depression, they decided they could not do without a car. They bought a used 1932 Model B Ford to replace the Model T.

Henry Ford had stopped production of the original Model B back before the Model T came out. But in 1931, to bolster flagging sales, he revamped the old Model A and from it built a new Model B, which could be fitted with either of two types of motors — the old four-cylinder motor or the new eight-cylinder, or V-8, motor.

The V-8 was the first real hot-rod car to hit American streets. Gangsters loved them. "It's a treat to drive this car," wrote Public Enemy Number One, John Dillinger, to Ford. Clyde Barrow sent Ford a similar testimonial, and when in 1934 he and Bonnie Parker died in Louisiana in their V-8 Fordor Deluxe under a hail of fire from lawmen, a local Ford dealer called to remove the car cranked the motor at first try, despite 107 bullet and buckshot holes in its body.

Bonnie and Clyde sometimes hid out north of Plum Ridge not too far from Nacogdoches. But it is doubtful that their endorsement motivated Corbett to choose the Model B roadster, which he and Fannie drove until after World War II. He always seemed much too practical.

And yet, sometimes he hummed a song made popular by Jimmie Rodgers, the railroad man's musician. It was called "Moonlight and Skies," and later on I heard some of the words on a record:

My pal's name was Blackie, a lad with true heart.
A robbery we planned, so decided to start.
I went to my darling, with tears in her eyes,
She said, Daddy don't leave me, your moonlight and skies.
I laughed at her pleading, youth must have its ways.
I says, I'll be back in a couple of days. . . .

I remember seeing the roadster when I was young. It sat down by the pasture fence near the barn at Pa Graham's place where Corbett and Fanny then lived. It had lost some of its parts to other uses. Weeds had grown up around it, and the tires had long since rotted on the wheels.

14   **Hard Times and Little Animals**

It is not these well-fed long-haired men that I fear,
But the pale and the hungry-looking.
Plutarch, *Lives, Antony*

The Great Depression missed me by a few years. Even so, growing up shortly thereafter showed me the strategies my parents and
grandparents had used to weather leaner years than mine. Of course, at
the time I never made the connection between the grown-ups' ways of
doing things and the avoidance of poverty. It occurred to me only later,
after I had encountered people who earned a comparable wage but
seemed irreversibly dependent on food stamps and unemployment
checks.

Looking back, I believe one of the greatest bastions against poverty
in those days was what sociologists today would call the extended family. Within this institution of grandparents, parents, kids, and dogs, traditional ways of "making do" had filtered down from generations past.
New skills didn't replace old ones; they complemented them. Shared
money, tools, and houses bridged an individual's temporary bad luck.
Not least, the family provided copious supplies of motivation, in part

because everyone viewed himself or herself as unique and necessary in the war on poverty.

I believe people took pride in their specialties. Boose brought in paychecks and built our furniture, Corbett furnished hog meat and a tractor, and Versie and Fannie washed the clothes, cooked, and canned the garden produce. Early on, my brother and I became the predators of the little animals.

Knowledge handed down by Corbett and Boose got Jack and me started, even before we grew old enough to carry guns. You could get a redbird with a rattrap baited with corn and set atop a fence post or with a slingshot if you were lucky. A good rain dampened the leaves so you could sneak near enough to whack an armadillo with a hickory club. You can twist a rabbit out of a hollow tree or log with a forked switch, Boose told us, but it proved so messy I did it only once.

After the .22's came into our lives, we learned the true value of our dogs. The only animals more easily hunted without them were gray squirrels in dense stands of timber and rabbits at night. Raccoons, opossums, and fox squirrels proved far easier to find with the help of better noses than ours.

We trained a succession of feist dogs — Bounce and Squeeze were the best ones — to become fox squirrel specialists. During school years six through twelve, a Saturday's walk through the longleaf woods would often yield a legal limit of those delicious animals. I remember weighing squirrel carcasses on Nama's meat scale to estimate what I had contributed to the family's food supply.

Several rules for working with a hunting dog turned out later to be instructive for tackling problems with human partners. First, make some attempt to start with one that demonstrates an inclination to work. Second, don't reward them too much; I ruined my dog Lady by petting her every time she came to me, and soon she did nothing but sit around and wait for praise. Scold them a little when they bark up the wrong tree but praise them when they do a good job. Most important, recognize that it's mainly you who's being trained by them and not the other way around.

By helping gather family food, Jack and I simply repeated what kids had been doing for thousands of years, I guess. Maybe that's why it felt so good. The genes knew best.

But our predatory ways posed problems I didn't think much about

132

*Hard
Times
and
Little
Animals*

until later. The "start" button gave a greater thrill than the "stop" button. Our predecessors had found this out, too, and by the time Jack and I set out to harvest food from the woods, only the small animals remained.

During my early teens, I followed a monthly column by Carlos Vinson in the *Farm Journal*. He sometimes talked about hunting or trapping wild animals. "Possums Day or Night," said the caption one month, and it opened up a new realm of possibilities.

"I refuse to cook a possum," my mother said in a tone that sounded final. "You'll have to talk to Mama about that."

"All right," said Fannie. "I'll cook him. As long as you get him out of a persimmon tree or some other place far away from dead cows and other garbage."

Opossums smell bad under any circumstance, and maybe that's why Corbett instructed me to let the carcass "air out" on the rooftop overnight. By the time Nama had baked it for three hours encircled with sweet potatoes, it smelled good and looked delicious. After tasting it, I decided squirrels were better and soon lost enthusiasm for hunting possum. But there was that time later when a group of friends and I stewed one we found trapped in a campground garbage can. That cured me forever.

When you're young, you seldom ask how adults know things. Not until years later did I speculate that Nama's willingness to cook the opossum and also her recipe must have come down with family traditions from harder times. A letter in that shoe box of memorabilia helped confirm that, at least to my satisfaction. Addressed to Fannie's father, S. F., in Texas, it had come from his mother in Cairo, Georgia, in 1874, in the depths of the Reconstruction that followed the Civil War.

> Dear Son,
>
> We were proud to hear that you were all well. . . . You spoke of hard times there. From what you say things are about like they are here. Provisions are high. Bacon is worth from 10 to 11 ct. [per pound], flour 9 to 10, corn 15, pork 10, beef more. . . . Major [S. F.'s uncle] has caught 20 opossums lately. . . . You wanted to know if we ever thought of coming to Texas. I see no chance. . . .

Georgia's animals had been exposed to Anglo settlers longer than those in Texas had been. The big animals in Georgia likely had been scarce for some time. Georgians coming to Texas would repeat what they had done in Georgia.

In 1884 the Texas Game, Fish, and Oyster Commission reported:

> At one time in the early days, Texas furnished without cost an abundance of fish and game. The streams abounded with the choicest varieties of the finny tribe, and the prairies and mots of timber with buffalo, deer, antelope, etc., while the lakes and ponds here and there were covered with geese, ducks, and other water fowl. But now all is changed. The sportsman is poorly rewarded for his long tramps over hill and prairie, and the fisherman returns from the rivers with a feeling of disappointment and disgust.

A half century after Reconstruction faded, another hard-times period emerged. The Great Depression people called it, and once again rural people searched the crannies of the woods with their guns and dogs. The number of people in Texas had multiplied since Reconstruction, and their arsenals had become more effective.

Halfway through the depression, the U.S. government's Biological Survey initiated a program to combat the wildlife depletion lamented by Texas legislators. The survey's director set up a program of cooperative training and research in nine states, including Texas. It started in 1935.

134

*Hard
Times
and
Little
Animals*

Texas A&M College collaborated with the federal government to establish the Texas Cooperative Wildlife Research Unit. They hired Walter P. Taylor of the Biological Survey to run it. Taylor, already known for his studies of rodents and rabbits and their effects on cattle grazing in Arizona, seemed especially suited to the task at hand. He possessed a strong conservation ethic, experience with mammals of a size range still common in Texas, and a dedication to field investigation.

Taylor's first graduate assistant, Dan Lay, finished his university studies in 1938 and went immediately into the woods of East Texas to find out what was happening to the wild animals. He trapped opossums and raccoons on given acreages to estimate their abundances. He questioned people to find out how many animals they trapped and shot. He added up the numbers and estimated the impacts of hunting and trapping.

In those days, small game, fish, and bullfrogs contributed appreciably to the tables set by country housewives. Rural people, who made up a substantial proportion of the total population in East Texas, searched the woods for meat to supplement a diet of corn, sweet potatoes, black-eyed peas, and collards. Conservation had not found its way into their habits or even their vocabularies.

By 1938 Lay had collected some data on small animals and their use by people. Opossums received a lot more attention then than they did after the depression ended. Lay wrote:

> A questionnaire answered recently by all the Negro enrollees in the Civilian Conservation Corps at the Lufkin and New Waverly camps showed that 57.6 percent of 2,098 Negroes living in eastern Texas eat an average of 4.9 opossums to the family a year. . . . Some white persons also eat opossums.

You could not only eat opossums, you could get money for their skins. Fur coats had come in style, though it seems doubtful that the catalogs called them "possum."

"This species [opossum] ranks as [the] most important source of fur income in Texas because of its abundance and wide distribution," Lay announced in 1938 on the front page of the newly created *Monthly Bulletin of the Texas Game, Fish, and Oyster Commission*. The article continued:

> All facts available on the status of coon and mink indicate that the trapping season on these species should be closed for at least three years. The mink and coon are valuable sources of income to trappers in the few scattered spots where they occur. Yet they are now so scarce that the lowly opossum ranks as the most important source of fur income in the state.

The next year in the *Monthly Bulletin*, Lay provided numbers to show the value of fur to depression-era trappers:

> A survey made by the Texas Cooperative Wildlife Research Unit in Walker County in eastern Texas showed that the 1936–37 fur crop

paid $57 to the average trapper. Compared with the average annual per capita farm income for eastern Texas of $176, this fur check received by one-tenth of the rural families had an important place in the economic and social structure of the region. . . . Those trappers fortunate enough to have good coon and mink territory made as much as $250 that winter.

Coon hides brought $2.50. No wonder coons and minks seemed about to follow the deer and turkeys to near extirpation. A dollar bought a lot in those days. Opossums held their own only by being prolific breeders.

A predator that has grown abundant on the land becomes especially fearsome to the little animals it consumes when other sources for its livelihood dry up. Depression's children scrapping for a living behaved no differently than other predators. Lay wrote:

> In eastern Texas, more trapping is done in years of economic stress when lumber mills and oil fields are partly or entirely shut down. Men otherwise too busy to trap locate their old traps, buy a few new ones, or hunt with dogs. Whatever they get for the fur is welcomed. Such trapping and hunting usually are done on land owned by others. Most of the extensive holdings of the lumber companies are not fenced and are open to unrestricted trapping. This has helped to bring about general scarcity of the most valuable species, such as coon and mink.
>
> The supplementary income which is received during December and January from the sale of furs keeps many families off relief rolls. No fortunes in Texas are built on the fur resource; instead, the income from fur goes . . . into the pockets of the people who need it most.

136
*Hard
Times
and
Little
Animals*

Finally, the depression ended. Young men left the woods and went off to war. Money gradually became easier to get. Small animals multiplied, and bigger ones cautiously edged out of secret places, making tracks where none had been seen for a decade or more. The Texas Game, Fish, and Oyster Commission began trapping deer in the Hill Country and hauling them in to restock East Texas.

In early winter of 1943 Corbett killed a big buck. He and Boose had ridden Dan and Stepper, Corbett's pair of sorrel geldings, from

Peachtree north toward the Angelina River to look for hogs. Near Hog Creek, the deer jumped up, and Corbett felled him with the second shot from his .22 Special. They brought the deer home lashed behind the saddle.

Years later, my mother said, "It was the first deer I remember Daddy shooting. I had never seen a deer before, except a pet deer someone had when I was a kid. We always lived in the woods, and I guess if there had been many deer I'd have seen one."

I have an early childhood memory of a horse coming home at twilight with a monstrous buck aboard. Whether it's a two-year-old's actual recollection of the deer Corbett killed in 1943 or a vision planted later by stories told and retold is hard to say. Jack still has the antlers nailed to the wall on his porch.

For me, turkeys made the jump from legend to reality in the middle fifties, more than a decade after Corbett killed the buck. It happened one spring day when we were coming home from feeding cattle.

By this time Corbett and Fannie had moved to live next door to us, in the Peachtree hammock. Pa Graham's place two miles to the north stood vacant. But Corbett's cattle still roamed the longleaf pinelands north of there, and I would sometimes go there with him and Fannie to check on them.

The cattle came to salt and feed at the edge of a deserted field adjacent to Pa Graham's place. Here, at an abandoned homesite we called Old Viney's, the last vestige of land that had been rich enough to farm dropped off to the longleaf pinelands that reached toward the Angelina bottom. Corbett always parked beside a large sycamore tree that overlooked a scattering of fence posts, rusted wire, and weathered boards.

If the special horn he had put on his '49 Ford pickup did not bring the cattle within a quarter hour or so, he would call them with a high-pitched yodel. It carried down across the hills toward Hog Creek and the Angelina bottom. How far the cows could hear it I do not know, but we sometimes waited thirty or forty minutes before we heard the cowbell coming.

This day we had fed the cows and started home. I stood in the pickup bed holding the front boards of the cattle frame; the wind felt good as the truck gathered speed. A movement by the woodland edge a hundred yards away caught my attention. I looked and saw a critter with neck outstretched race to hide itself behind a growth of young

137
Hard
Times
and
Little
Animals

loblolly pines that had crept into the opening. I pounded on the pickup roof. Corbett stopped.

"It looked like a turkey," I almost shouted. "It sure was fast."

"We're too far from anybody's house to see a tame turkey," Corbett said. "Point out where it was, and we'll go look for tracks."

As we left the truck, Corbett ruminated, "It's been quite a few years since I've heard anybody talk of seeing turkeys, but you never can tell."

A cattle trail paralleled the rusted barbed wire where the blackjack oaks and buckeye bushes leaned into the opening.

"Look here," Corbett said, pointing to a scuff mark in the sandy path. "I believe it is a turkey, sure enough."

I can see those tracks even now. They looked like a chicken's tracks but bigger, and I had to stretch my legs to reach between them.

We went home, and the next day Corbett rustled about in a pile of scrap lumber and found an inch-wide piece of cedar. With a three-quarter-inch bit he drilled a row of overlapping holes in its twelve-inch length to make a sort of narrow box. He whittled and smoothed the inside of the box with his pocketknife. He made a lid, which he rounded on the underside and attached loosely to one end of the opening with a screw.

"What's that?" I asked, but he seemed engrossed in scraping the sidewalls thinner. He moved the lid from side to side, so that it rasped across the edges of the box. He moved his mouth, as if teaching it to speak.

138
*Hard
Times
and
Little
Animals*

"Here," he said at last. "Work it like this."

"Eow! Eow!" it yelped as he rubbed the lid across one edge of the opening.

"What's it for?" I asked again, trying with not much luck to make a sound like he had made.

"Go call a turkey," he said, and left me sitting on a stump, searching for the motion that would make it say "Eow!"

Years later, while leafing through an outdoor magazine, I saw the image of Corbett's handmade box advertised for sale. The original cedar-box turkey call, it said. I still have the one Corbett made. It is the original.

15 Poppin' Johnny

. . . There appeared a chariot of fire, and horses of fire . . . and Elijah went up by a whirlwind into heaven.

2 Kings 2:11

Mr. Ford's car no doubt had eased the depression's impact on Corbett and Fannie, but it had also planted the seeds of a vague unrest. Walking no longer felt fast enough. Old Queenie began to seem inadequate. Corbett took to leafing through all the farm magazines he could get his hands on and looking at the tractors. Then, in the early 1940s, the depression's bonds loosened, and the desire generated by the advertisements escalated.

Mechanization of farming in America had accelerated dramatically between the start of the twentieth century and the beginning of the depression. Internal combustion engines fueled by cheap oil could operate more cost-effectively than animal power. Farmers during this period rapidly increased their use of machines and consequently their crop production.

Because fewer horses and mules had to be kept and fed, more acreage became available for growing human food. In the 1920s large surpluses in farm production caused the unit value of crops to drop. Many people dependent on farming for an income felt driven to buy a tractor and plow more land.

After the depression hit, farmers really felt the impact of growing too much wheat, corn, and cotton. Not only did they continue to suffer because of surplus crop production, food exports plummeted, and Americans in cities cut back on their consumption of farm products. Rayon fibers made from oil replaced cotton for many uses. But the costs for buying and maintaining tractors and other farm machinery did not fall accordingly.

The exodus from farm to urban areas that had started earlier accelerated as the sizes of tractors increased and the price of food dropped. In eastern Texas, cities burgeoned as the children of backwoods farmers flocked to jobs in lumber mills, oil refineries, and retail stores. Corbett's brothers moved to town.

Corbett and Fannie, like most farmers, endured the depression by cutting their consumption of things that cost money. But, unlike many, they had options other than selling crops — the timber industry still needed flatheads and saw filers, fish still could be caught from the Angelina River, and acorns still fed hogs and game that could be hunted in the hinterlands. A diversity of resources in a thinly settled region insulated them from the breakdown in the farm economy.

Their family circumstances helped to keep expenses down. My mother, Versie, was their only child; other couples of their generation found themselves obliged to feed and clothe broods of six, eight, or even ten. Custom also made it normal for extended families to share the same roof. Thus, when in 1940 Versie married, she and my father lived at first with Corbett and Fannie, helping run the farm and bring in money.

In late 1941 Pearl Harbor and World War II galvanized the country into action. The war brought a change in the fortunes of the farmer. Food exports escalated to feed American soldiers and Allied countries, and jobs proliferated to feed the war machine. Things looked so good by 1944 that Corbett bought a tractor.

Alas, it was not a Ford. Henry Ford had experimented at building farm tractors as early as 1905, and the Fordson tractor had first appeared on the market in 1917, in response to demands created by World War I. These tractors had flooded the market in the 1920s, but cars ultimately proved more profitable to Henry Ford than tractors. The last of his Fordson tractors to be made in North America came off the line in 1928. Other tractors took their place in the thirties — Farmall, McCormick-Deering, Massey-Harris, John Deere.

The Deere Company in 1933 had tested a tractor unique in motor design — it had two large cylinders instead of the four smaller ones commonly in use. This allowed it to operate on fuel oil, kerosene, cheap gasoline, or other low-grade fuels. By World War II the John Deere tractor, or Poppin' Johnny, so-called because of the distinctive "pop-pop" of the engine, had, like Ford's Model T, built a reputation for simplicity and easy maintenance.

The farm dealer from San Augustine, fifty miles north of Jasper, hauled Corbett's new tractor to Peachtree. He unloaded it at a cutbank by the road about halfway up the hill between the Old Kirby Main Line and Pa Graham's sandhill farm. Corbett's hands trembled as he climbed aboard.

What a beauty! "John Deere" stood out in yellow letters on the leaf-green shroud above the motor. The front and rear wheels were built to straddle a row of corn or cotton. The huge rear tires with inch-high cleats looked like they could take you anywhere.

Corbett hung the horses' harnesses on nails beneath the corncrib roof. He put away the trace chains and singletrees. He stacked the horse-drawn turning plow and the Georgia stocks to gather dust. He hooked the new plows to the belly of the tractor and watched them rise and fall as he moved the shiny lever that powered the hydraulic lift.

A wonderful beast it was. You fed it only when it worked. It never tired. It could plow the fields, uproot stumps, and, with a belt hooked to its power takeoff, run machines of many kinds.

He took it into the piney woods and bottomlands where roads were few and bad. It chugged with scarce a strain through sandy ruts and mud-filled hollows that would bog the Model B. Off the roads it straddled pine knots, pushed through brush, and jumped small logs.

I soon grew old enough to marvel at the tractor. When Corbett parked it in the open, he capped the upright pipe that vented the exhaust with an empty can to keep out rain. To me, the tractor's greatest feat was the ease with which it tossed the can high into the air when the engine started up.

When I was young, we occasionally hauled fence posts from the

A wonderful beast it was. Corbett's grandsons on his tractor in the late 1940s.

woods in a two-wheeled trailer Corbett pulled behind the tractor. The best posts came from logs or snags of "lighter" pine — the resin-filled heartwood of longleaf. They would resist rot for many decades, even where the ground stayed wet.

Corbett and Fannie would cut the logs to six-foot lengths with a crosscut saw lubricated with kerosene to keep the blade clear of resin. We would split the logs — I helped a little — with factory wedges made of iron and longer ones called "gluts" Corbett shaped from dogwood. I would come home after those trips with my hands and clothes blackened with pitch.

Latter-day turpentiners swept the pinewoods clean of post material in the 1950s. They blasted out the ancient stumps and hauled them and any heartwood logs they could find to market for their resin.

The tractor seemed invincible, but it had a special weakness. With the body high off the ground and the short length of the axles, it could overbalance easily. Corbett found this out early on; he once had to call Boose for help when the tractor teetered on the down side of a terrace in the field. But it was easy to forget this problem when the tractor perked along on level ground with such assurance.

One day Corbett decided he would like to spend more time fishing. But he had no boat. The thing to do was make one. So he hooked the trailer to the tractor, loaded up the axes and the crosscut saw, and recruited Boose to help. They would make two boats, one for each of them. They headed for the Angelina bottom, to a stand of cypress trees he knew about.

To reach the trees they wanted, they had to cross a creek named Willow Branch a quarter mile or so above its juncture with the Angelina River. Beyond this creek, they steered their way among the water oaks and hickories. The bottom hardwoods still stood tall and far apart in those days — the dam had not been built upstream, and the river still overflowed its banks in spring and drowned the pines and other seedlings intolerant of flooding. A short way farther on near Hog Creek, in a little slough, they cut the cypress logs they needed and loaded them onto the trailer.

Soon after they began the trip back home, they met with near disaster. To recross Willow Branch with the laden trailer, Corbett had to angle down the bank. As he slowly moved the tractor downslope, it leaned farther and farther to one side and then started to tip. Corbett realized then that he had to turn the front end more toward the creek.

You could steer the John Deere tractor to a great extent by braking. It had two brakes side by side, one for the left rear wheel and one for the right. If you wanted to turn sharply left, you pressed your foot on the left-wheel brake, and vice versa if you wanted to turn right.

Corbett quickly stamped the brake — the wrong one. The uphill wheel locked, and the front end of the tractor swung away from the creek. The green and yellow beast slowly tumbled to its side, tossing driver, tool kit, and all the other unattached parts into the creek. As luck would have it, Corbett fell free of the tractor, which stayed on its side and rolled no further.

After briefly surveying the situation, Corbett left Boose with the helpless tractor and walked the five miles home for a chain. When he arrived back at the crossing, they secured one end of the chain onto the down side of the tractor, drew the chain over the tractor's top, and wrapped the other end around the bottom of a stout pole that was forked at the top. By twisting the forked end of the pole to take up slack in the chain and prying with the pole around the trunk of a tree, they managed to jack the tractor upright.

They brought the logs home and had them sawed into lumber at the sawmill. With a few brass screws and a little tar, they made two fine boats that they paddled up and down the Angelina for many years' fishing.

You had to watch yourself around that tractor, all right. It didn't back its ears in warning like a horse does before it kicks. Once Corbett broke his leg when he tried to start the engine with his foot; the crank kicked back and caught him on the shin.

The tractor had some lessons to teach about technology. When machines work, they let you do great things with little effort. But they can also take you farther out on a limb than you would normally go, and when they break down, you may find it harder to get back. Corbett in his time seldom ventured far enough out that he couldn't get back with a little ingenuity and a few simple tools.

One fine December morning in 1959 I ate breakfast early, took my single-shot Winchester .22 from the closet, and walked up the road to Corbett's barn. He had invited me to go hog hunting.

I found him hooking the trailer to the tractor. His dogs, Tige and Midge, were going wild. He slid his Winchester .22 Special underneath the tarp in the trailer bottom, I climbed in with the dogs, and he wheeled the tractor around.

Pop! Pop! Pop! Pop! went the engine as we turned out the lane and picked up speed. We went north on the sand and clay Peachtree road. I sat on the floor of the trailer, facing backward with my collar turned up, and stuffed my hands inside my coat pockets. The two dogs leaned their heads over the sides and shoved their noses into the wind.

Shortly after we passed Pa Graham's place, vacant since Corbett and Fannie had moved nearer our house several years before, he slowed the tractor. Tige and Midge perked their ears. Corbett waved his hand.

"Go ahead!" he called, and the dogs hit the ground at a run.

As we wound our way through the woods on thin ruts, the dogs would disappear for a time, then reappear, first on one side and then on the other. Thirty or forty minutes later, Corbett pulled the tractor to a stop and switched the motor off. We had come near a branch of Hog Creek, and a hundred yards or so through the red oak and longleaf pine trees, you could see the bay and wax myrtle bushes at the head of a baygall. We had not seen the dogs for some time.

Hog Creek ran right through the middle of the country Corbett's hogs inhabited. Kirby and other lumber companies owned most of this land but in those days allowed free access. Local people had agreed on a set of unwritten rules about whose hogs occupied which pieces of land; I never understood these rules entirely except that the history of use played an important part.

Each spring Corbett took his dogs into the woods to round up hogs. This required not only a horse but also pens located at strategic places. These pens — small, hog-proof corrals of poles and net wire — had wings expanding outward from their gates. With the help of dogs and horse, Corbett found each bunch of hogs and drove them to the nearest pen, where the wings helped him to funnel them inside.

Corbett saw which young hogs were his by the earmarks of their mothers. Once he had them penned, he roped the unmarked ones, pulled them squealing to the fence and, up above the popping jaws of sows, cut his mark into their ears with his pocketknife. With the same knife, he'd make "meat hogs" of the small pigs — that is, castrate them — and bob their tails. No one ate uncastrated males; the smell of boar meat cooking would drive you from the kitchen.

A pig cannot be roped as easily as a calf. Its neck is short and thick, and even a limber cotton rope will come right off unless you also get a front leg in the loop. Corbett could rope small pigs from horseback, some who knew him said. He'd pull them off the ground and mark them from the saddle. I never found it easy roping pigs, even in the pen; the old sow rushing at the fence made me nervous.

On that December morning I watched Corbett as we waited. He finally straightened up and cocked his head. I couldn't hear a thing.

"There they are," he said, waving his arm in the general direction of the creek. "Over yonder. We'll leave the tractor here."

When we drew near the baying dogs, Corbett slowed his pace. He set each foot with care into the rustling leaves and with his hand pushed the branches to the side so they wouldn't scratch against his overalls and denim jumper. I hung back a ways to keep from getting slapped when he let the branches go.

The dogs kept up a steady barking, but I couldn't see them for the tangle of the briars and bushes. Corbett dropped down and began to crawl through the brush with his rifle in his right hand. Soon he disappeared from sight ahead of me.

Suddenly the barking stopped. I counted seconds — one, two,

The last great beasts. Corbett presides over the butchering of some of the last of his woods hogs, taken from near Hog Creek in the early 1960s.

three, four. The rifle cracked. A great rustling of leaves commenced and led away down the baygall; a snapping of sticks and a snarling and growling of dogs issued from the thicket just ahead.

When I reached the scene, a mud black hog lay on its side. Corbett put away his pocketknife, and Midge lapped at the blood pumping from a small hole just off-center underneath the sow's neck. I leaned close and saw a tiny bullet hole in the left side of its head, halfway between the eye and the base of the ear.

"We'll drag her out to open woods," Corbett said. "Then I'll get the tractor."

It was late that afternoon when I got my chance. The dogs had bayed another bunch of hogs, and Corbett had eased up and shot one. I was close enough to see this time, and when the others broke and ran, Corbett whistled at the dogs and waved his hand.

"Git 'em!" he yelled, and the dogs sped away.

"I'll take care of this one," he said as I came up. "You catch up with the dogs and shoot that other big one. He's a meat hog, you'll see by his stubby tail."

The barking rapidly grew fainter, so I took off at a lope. I knew these woods fairly well by now, so didn't worry much when the dogs headed down toward the Angelina bottom. They had gone about a mile, always out of sight ahead of me, when I heard their barking change. I knew they had brought the hogs to bay.

With the baying of the dogs just ahead, I slowed to catch my breath and get my bearings. Soon I spotted a familiar ridge that came down to the creek bank. Hole-in-the-Rock lay just a little way down the creek.

Shortly I saw a movement through the screen of brush and tree trunks. Midge and Tige faced a dingy black-and-yellow shape. The hog looked big; somehow the dogs had known to follow him and not the smaller ones that must have split off earlier. I saw the inch-long tail.

As I moved to get a better view, the hog swung around to face me; he had heard or seen my movement. I waited, hoping he would turn his head.

"Don't shoot between the eyes," Corbett always said. "It'll flatten on the skull."

Minutes passed, and the Hog Creek bottom darkened. The sun had left the trees, and the sky had clouded over. Sunset could not be far away. Still the old hog would not turn his head. The dogs barked hoarsely.

I raised the .22, aiming right between his eyes. The sights seemed fuzzy already; I shouldn't wait much longer. I cocked the rifle. How could a bullet bounce off a hog's skull from this close a range? If I shot just right there. . . . I touched the trigger.

Pop! The noise startled me. The hog dropped instantly, and I lowered the gun. Well, that shows you what a little .22 short can do.

Suddenly the hog lunged to his feet, and I jammed my hand into my pocket for another cartridge. As I loaded it into the chamber of the gun, I saw the chunky shape disappear into the brush with the dogs close behind.

They went several hundred yards before they stopped again. This time I took my time sneaking up, despite my pounding heart. Shoot right there, on a line between the eye and ear. I could barely see the rifle sights, but the hog was close. This time he went down for good but thrashed around a lot even after I had cut a ragged hole behind one cheek and blood gurgled out.

I ran into Corbett a short distance back up the creek; he had come to look for me. It had turned pitch dark by the time we relocated the hog, looped a rope around his snout behind a stick put crossways in back of his tusks, and hung him to an overhanging tree limb. It took a lot of heaving and pulling on the rope to get the carcass off the ground.

"He'll go three hundred pounds," Corbett said. "I'll have to gut him now or he'll sour. We'll come back for him tomorrow."

We had no light, and I wondered what we'd do. But Corbett not only took out the insides as cleanly as if it had been daylight, he went straight back to the tractor without a pause. On the way I looked in vain for my hand before my face.

It started raining in the night, and by morning clay spots on the roads squished underfoot like axle grease. But the John Deere tractor plowed through foot-deep ruts, flattened brush when it turned off the road, and chugged up to the hog without a hesitation.

For me, that was the last great Angelina beast. By then the stock law had reached our woods. It required that livestock owners keep their animals behind a fence, and free-roaming hogs became fair game to anyone. It was ushered in by the children of those who had fled the countryside in the depression. They had no use for animals running loose; their food came from grocery stores.

16 **Wires**

. . . all day I climb myself
Bowlegged up those damned poles   rooster-heeled in all
Kinds of weather . . .

.   .   .   .

And this is the house I pass through on my way
To power and light.
James Dickey, "Power and Light"

In 1950 the Rural Electric Administration cut a right-of-way, put in poles, and strung wires up the sand hill to Pa Graham's place where Corbett and Fannie watched after my aging great-grandfather. An electrician came and installed lights. REA had come at last to the hinterlands.

My brother and I felt the change immediately. When we stayed overnight there, we no longer got to argue over who would blow out the kerosene lamp at bedtime, except when the electricity went out. I had appreciated the flame inside the lamp's steeple-shaped globe more than the new bulb of light that never wavered and could not be lighted with a match or doused with a puff.

Not long after that, Corbett and Fannie decided to build a new house. People often moved out of their old homes when electricity came, partly because the frontier style of house did not fit the applications of electrical power. Electric fans for cooling favored low ceilings and all-enclosed houses rather than the old high-ceiling houses with a dogtrot breezeway through the middle. Old houses and water wells had not been built to accommodate indoor bathrooms and electric water pumps.

So Corbett cleared a space among the hardwoods two miles to the south, just up the road from where I lived with my father, mother, and brother. He and Fannie began building a house foundation. They refrained from telling Pa.

When Pa Graham eventually learned about their plan to move, he rebelled. Perhaps he viewed it as a rejection of his way of life, of the house and farm he had built. He pouted. Someone whispered that he came at Corbett with a knife.

In any case, he never lived with them in the new electrified house. He spent his last few years in town, at first with his other children, and then they moved him to an old folks' home. They left his house staring vacantly out at its sandy yard. It slowly fell into disrepair.

≈In high school our science class made a trip to the Jasper electric generating plant. I remember seeing a couple of gigantic wheels whirring inside a frame but cannot recall learning much about their purpose. Though electricity had demonstrated its importance to me by that time, knowing that the bedside radio Jack and I shared would work when I plugged it in seemed sufficient.

Later I grew more curious. We learned in history class that Ben Franklin flew a kite during a storm to experiment with electricity and in physics class that Michael Faraday made electricity by rotating a copper disc between the poles of a magnet. Engineers built on Faraday's discovery to rotate huge metal coils in a powerful magnetic field. That explained the wheels in the Jasper electric plant.

I eventually learned that those wires snaking through our woods from pole to pole performed the real magic. They transported power by some process too deep to fully understand, substituting for trucks and pipelines that had previously transported oil, gas, and coal. They brought power from the plant to the outlet in the living room.

The final lesson came when I got a good look at what lay at the other end of the wire. That happened in 1971, near Fairfield, Texas, over a hundred miles west of Jasper. I had taken a temporary job at a

The old house tumbled down when they moved away. Pa Graham's house in 1971.

coal mine recently opened by the Texas Utilities Company out of Dallas.

The project map showed several square miles of post-oak woods and abandoned farmland scheduled to be mined. The power plant had already reached its seven-story height near a lake that had been built to cool the plant's coal-fired generators. Machines a mile away stripped soil and timber to get at the seam of coal that lay beneath.

A supervisor took me to a dragline that towered above the trees. A yellow extension cord thick as a man's leg led to the machine from some power source beyond a screen of post-oaks. The dragline moved slowly, eerily silent except for the whirring of fans that cooled its electric heart. Two stories off the ground a man in the glassed-in cab controlled a crane longer than a football field and a bucket that could swallow the Dallas Cowboys football team, substitutes and all. The bucket moved dirt.

In the nearby pit just opened up, the maw of another machine scooped up the coal exposed by the dragline and loaded it into a truck with wheels higher than my reach. Other trucks stood in line. Each one carried enough coal to fill a modest house, and each when filled lumbered away to the pulverizer, which prepared the coal for burning at the generating plant.

Wires led from the generators. Running from tower to tower like shiny jump ropes at rest, they disappeared into the distance toward the network company workers called the grid, which fed Texas cities, towns, and rural places. They stretched toward a dream of limitless power and light.

As alluring as the magic in the mammoth hunter's blade, the electricity enticed people to build their livelihoods on that which they could not control or comprehend. They gained convenience. They lost another piece of independence.

Electricity made life easier for Fannie. Soon Corbett brought home an electric refrigerator, then a freezer. She didn't have to rush as much now when they butchered hogs; late at night she could put the pans of meat in the icebox and wait until the next day to finish making sausage. Putting pork, black-eyed peas, and creamed corn into the deep freeze was a great relief from canning.

Corbett found an old electric motor and fixed it up with belts and gears to run the sausage grinder. Now they didn't have to turn the crank by hand; that speeded up the butchering. Soon Fannie built herself a bigger business selling pork.

Several years before, they had bought a 1949 Ford pickup. Now, each fall and winter during hog-killing time, Fannie would load the sausage, bacon, hams, and hogshead cheese into the truck and drive to Jasper. She parked at the courthouse square and sat on the tailgate, weighing out portions to customers as they came around. She was always careful to drape old bedsheets over everything to keep out flies.

One fall the health inspector came around. He told her she could no longer carry out her business this way. Soon thereafter, word got out to her customers that she had taken to parking back in the alley.

By selling pork, Fannie made enough money that Corbett could afford to keep his cows, says my mother. I didn't know anything about her profits, but I haven't tasted an equal to her sausage since.

The stock law came close on the heels of REA. To comply with the stock law required that people keep their cows and hogs behind fences. The law put an official end to the generations-old tradition among rural folks who had paid scant attention to the wanderings of their livestock.

In practice, the penalty for failure to maintain animal-proof fences was forfeiture of ownership. Not long after the stock law came into effect, a few cows somehow escaped the three-thousand-acre pinewoods pasture where Corbett kept his herd; they ended up in the county "pond-pen" and were eventually sold to "pay for their keep." Despite their being branded, Corbett never heard about it until too late. My father called it legal rustling and started a personal campaign to oust the county commissioners.

Woods hogs, of course, paid no attention to the three-strand barbed wire fence that enclosed the cattle. Soon a new tradition developed among those local people who had little respect for older ways: the only good hog is a dead hog. Because nearly all the Angelina country remained open to the public, Corbett foresaw the end of running hogs.

The year before the stock law went into effect, Corbett earmarked 480 pigs. That brought his total in the woods to around a thousand head, he guessed. He stopped marking hogs after that but worked hard then and in the next few years to kill for market all he could. Fannie sold a lot of meat.

The cows required a different strategy to meet the stock law. Corbett soon stopped repairing the rusty barbed wire fence that had kept his cows on the lumber company land that he had leased for a dollar's payment every year. He hauled some cows to auction in the back of the '49 Ford pickup fitted with a cattle frame, and he made plans to bring the remainder to Peachtree. He checked the Peachtree fence to make sure it would hold the cows.

Jack and I had helped build part of the fence around the fifty-acre pasture. Every five steps along the narrow right-of-way through the woods along the property line, we dug a posthole. The jaws of the digger sank easily into the loamy soil except when you hit a tree root. The posts, mostly of longleaf heartwood but sometimes of chinquapin or mulberry, had to be set in the holes and anchored firmly by filling in around them and tamping the soil with the end of a slim pole.

Corbett and Boose had decided to build the fence of net wire instead of barbed wire. It cost more but would hold hogs as well as cattle. We rolled it down the lane beside the posts, Corbett pulled it tight with the tractor, and we stapled it to the posts. The wires hummed when you tapped them with the hammer.

Up into the middle 1950s, hardwood trees of many kinds had covered nearly all fifty acres. My brother and I had played among and in the trees. The woods were great for squirrels and winter robins but not much good for cows.

In 1956 Corbett and Boose had put their heads together and decided that the hardwoods needed clearing. Corbett may have looked ahead and seen the stock law coming. They arranged to sell the better trees for timber, then to call in bulldozer operators. The government, under its land "improvement" program, had agreed to pay part of the cost of clearing.

First the loggers came with trucks and mules. The flatheads worked in teams of two with crosscut saws to fell the trees. The mules, likewise in pairs, pulled logs from the woods. With cant hooks the workers rolled the logs onto the truck up a ramp of poles leaned against the bed. The loggers took the best — for the third time in fifty years — and also the second best.

The mules seemed insignificant in strength when a few weeks later the Caterpillar tractors came. We heard two of the Cats growling at the trees one day when we came home from school. The saplings waved and cracked.

Thereafter, we raced from the school bus stop each afternoon to watch the yellow beasts at work. Their power seemed unlimited, but they had trouble with the largest beeches, uncut because the loggers had seen the squirrel holes in their trunks and knew that they were hollow. The Cats lifted up their blades to lean against the trunks and push; they dropped their blades to dig into the ground and break the roots. The effort disabled one machine, and we watched the welders' torches sparkling in the evening rain.

Soon the land stood bare of vegetation, seeming steeper than before. The trees lay piled in windrows, later setting winter nights ablaze when the grown-ups lit them with kerosene and a match. Next summer you could see that the ashes had added something to the dirt, because the corn we planted where the logs had burned grew twice as big as it did on the soil between the windrows.

Very soon the weeds and grass moved in. The land had forage fit for cows a few years later when Corbett brought them from the piney woods.

Livelihood had forced itself into a smaller space, but it didn't seem to matter much. Money flowed — to pay for Corbett's cows, for Fannie's dwindling loads of pork, and for Corbett's help in building houses. The old pinewoods cow pasture and other land toward the Angelina River still had no locks on the gates, and Corbett, Fannie, Jack, and I still went there fishing and hunting, picking grapes and mayhaws, or just riding in the truck.

Sometime during the late fifties Corbett's last horse, Dan, came down with colic. He wouldn't stand. Fannie stayed up all night holding his head in her lap, but he died anyway. His teammate Old Stepper's bones had bleached for several years in a little hollow in the pinewoods near Pa Graham's place.

In 1960 Corbett bought a new Ford, a four-door car. You couldn't haul animals, fence posts, firewood, or much of anything else in it, but there wasn't much that needed hauling by then anyway. They kept the old pickup, just in case.

Fannie got a washing machine, an electric iron, and a food mixer. Having all those gadgets didn't slow her down. When she ran out of work around the house, she would go with Corbett up into the woods. They still had the tractor.

She started tiring more in the early sixties. She would "give out" on a long walk. For some time there had been a sore spot on her forearm that wouldn't heal, but she had simply tied a rag around it and kept on working.

One day she went with Corbett up toward the Angelina River, and he got the tractor stuck. They stayed out nearly all night, and it exhausted her. Next day they drove to Houston to see a doctor, and he diagnosed the cancer she had had for many years.

She died in 1965, at home in Peachtree. Corbett, Versie, and Boose were there. It had been a good life, a long time since she'd had to worry with those awful briars.

17 Power Brokers

Power tends to corrupt . . .
J. E. E. Dalberg, First Baron Acton

By the middle 1960s Boose had acquired a reputation as the best cabinetmaker in Jasper County. A few months before Fannie died, he received an unusual request. The U.S. Army Corps of Engineers wanted him to build a speaker's podium.

This was to be no ordinary podium. It needed to be several inches higher than normal. More important, all parts must be clearly visible from the outside; there could be no hidden areas that might hide a bomb. The Corps of Engineers would use it when they dedicated the Sam Rayburn Dam and Reservoir on the Angelina River. The speaker who would stand behind the podium and give the dedication was the president of the United States, Lyndon Baines Johnson.

The dam and reservoir project had been funded in the main by federal tax dollars. It had, according to the Jasper newspaper, been "visualized" by three Texas politicians — Lyndon Johnson; the late Sam Rayburn, speaker of the U.S. House of Representatives; and local U.S.

Congressman Jack Brooks. Their vision, the paper said, "became a reality after years of national and local political struggle." Among the business interests, only the timber companies had objected.

Local chambers of commerce buzzed for weeks before the dedication. The Jasper "Sam Rayburn Dedication Committee on the Job" took shape. Officials committed themselves to come from all the region's counties — Jasper, Angelina, Sabine, Nacogdoches, San Augustine, Hardin, Tyler, Jefferson, Polk, Newton, Orange, and Liberty.

The Corps of Engineers, which had planned and built the dam, appointed Lt. Col. James H. Nash to take charge of the proceedings. Officers of regional governments and corporations filled lesser posts. Ceremonies would get under way at eight in the morning on May 8, 1965, fifteen miles north of Jasper at the east end of the dam.

Planners of the ceremony slated entertainment for the fifty thousand people expected to invade this sparsely settled pinewoods region. Hank Williams, Jr., singing star, and Miss Texas would appear, as would Stephen F. Austin University's Jazz Band, Lumberjack Band, and Twirl-O-Jack twirlers. Gordon Baxter, Beaumont media personality, would come as well.

Someone had arranged for the Alabama-Coushatti Indians to put on a dance. They had always been friendly with whites.

When the time came, Lyndon Johnson failed to show up. Instead, he gave a speech by phone from the White House. In the dedication he praised Sam Rayburn, dead four years come November, as his "teacher and counselor." Workers later set a bronze plaque in Texas red granite near the dam's powerhouse to commemorate the dedication; it contained a likeness of Rayburn's face.

The dedication culminated a familiar American political play: bringing home the bacon. Lyndon Johnson and Sam Rayburn had played the leading roles. They had been tutored in a frontier school that had learned the profits to be made by plowing, chopping, and digging at land.

The Johnson family came from Georgia in 1846 and settled down to eke a living from a thin-dirt farm near the Pedernales River west of Austin. More than half a century later, Sam Johnson, Lyndon's father, entered into politics to try to make a better living for his family. In

1907, when Sam rode a horse the sixty miles to Austin for his second term in the Texas legislature, he met, among the new faces in this thirtieth session, a twenty-four-year-old schoolteacher from Bonham named Sam Rayburn.

By his twelfth year, Lyndon Johnson often went with his father to Austin when the Texas legislature was in session. He heard stirring words confuse reality, and he saw his father hobnob with free-spending lobbyists from industry. He learned about power.

Early in his adult life, Lyndon acquired the knack of cultivating "political daddys." When at twenty-three he went to Washington as congressional secretary to the newly elected Richard Kleberg of the legendary King Ranch, he right away prodded Kleberg to introduce him to the senators and representatives from Texas. Soon President Franklin Roosevelt called Lyndon by name, and Johnson used FDR's influence in 1937 to win a seat for himself in the U.S. House of Representatives. Fellow politicians nicknamed him "Professional Son."

In 1948 Johnson decided to run for the U.S. Senate against Coke Stevenson, recent ex-governor of Texas. Robert Caro, a Johnson biographer, admired Stevenson's quietness and competence which, through his years of public service, had drawn the Texas people to him. In the Democratic primary for his second governor's race in 1944, Stevenson had carried all 254 counties in the state. Most Texans had made their place in life by working, and they admired a "doer."

By contrast, Johnson made his way by talking. In his campaign against Stevenson, to reach the people he flew from city to city in a helicopter and gave ringing speeches to the crowds that this flamboyant mode of entry generated. He cultivated agents of the Washington press, and through them harassed Stevenson with accusations. Robert Caro would later write that Johnson hired "whisperers" to infiltrate Texas small town coffee shops and public meetings, dropping rumors of Stevenson being a socialist and secretly dealing with organized labor.

Johnson won the race by eighty-seven votes out of about a million cast. Stevenson and many Texans were outraged. Accusations flew that Johnson had bought votes in South Texas, but nothing could be proved because the crucial ballot box had been "lost."

The defeat of Stevenson marked the end of an era, Robert Caro believed. Before this time, Texans had admired and supported those who did much but said little; now, a good number of them had listened to the talk and turned against their man of action. Performance and substance had given way to persuasion and image.

⤜Sam Rayburn proclaimed his mission in life in his first speech to the U.S. Congress on May 6, 1913: "It is . . . my sole purpose here to help enact such wise and just laws that our common country will by virtue of these laws be a happier and more prosperous country."

For forty-eight years he worked to his end. He and Coke Stevenson seemed to have had much in common.

Sam Rayburn's office had marked one of Lyndon Johnson's first stops in 1931 when he reached Washington as Kleberg's secretary. He soon found Rayburn to be not only already a political power but also a lonely bachelor. Rayburn quickly warmed to this fellow Texan who came around frequently; Mr. Sam, as the legislators called Rayburn, began to treat Lyndon like a son.

After Lyndon married in 1934, Rayburn's friendship with Johnson extended to his wife, Lady Bird. Over the years Mr. Sam adopted the Johnsons as the family he'd never known. When in 1940 Rayburn became Speaker of the House of Representatives, Lyndon's foresight was confirmed.

Sam Rayburn fell sick in the spring of 1961. Johnson came to sit beside the bed where he lay in the Baylor Medical Hospital in Dallas. When he died that fall on November 16, his life savings totalled $15,000. Some recalled an axiom coined by him: in politics, an honest man does not get rich.

On the other extreme, Lyndon Johnson had branched into numerous businesses from his point of vantage in Washington. When on the Senate Commerce Committee in 1952, he cleared a path to Johnson family ownership of a TV channel license in Austin, and in granting the permit the Federal Communications Commission barred others in the state from obtaining competitive licenses. Soon, with earnings from the TV station and a radio station, he ventured into oil, banking, real estate, and ranching. Caro notes that in 1941 Johnson had less than $1,000 in the bank; by the time he became president in 1963, his family's assets totalled around $20 million.

By 1965, wrote Beaumont newsman Gordon Baxter, Texas had "taken over" the U.S. government with the help of Lyndon Johnson and Sam Rayburn. These two old cronies, Baxter said, with their local apprentice-to-power Jack Brooks, were men of vision and clout. In the years of struggle to justify the building of the Sam Rayburn Dam, each reelection term Brooks had faced an opponent more powerful than the one before. But the public kept on reelecting Brooks, and soon it was too late to prevent the dam's construction.

The federal government justified the project's cost by showing that the area's rural electric cooperatives wanted the power and that communities on the lower Neches River needed the water for rice farming and industry. The U.S. Congress began appropriating money in 1955.

Official ground-breaking for major construction took place on Labor Day, 1957, with Congressman Jack Brooks as master of ceremonies. Jasper had a holiday for businesses and schools. Contractors lined up their machines.

Draftsmen drew the outlines of the future lake on maps, and the government sent men around to buy the property. For the landowners, it was all over but the dickering. By May 31, 1962, the *Jasper News-Boy* reported that the acquisition of the land by the government was 80 percent complete.

Two months later, the Corps of Engineers let bids for clearing sixty-seven thousand acres of land upstream of the dam. Something over a hundred square miles, this acreage would first have valuable timber cut and hauled away. Then worthless trees and brush would be cleared and burned. Three massive LeTourneau tree-crusher machines would be brought in to help.

A quarter century later, in 1987, the Corps of Engineers printed up a new edition of its pamphlet, *Sam Rayburn Dam and Reservoir*. The brochure tells about the history and the purpose of the project and spells out regulations for the use of project lands by the public.

"Do not damage or remove trees or plants," it says. "Protect the forest." Said Gordon Baxter in 1991:

After the shouting died down from the first struggle over its very existence, the development of Lake Sam Rayburn has proceeded

"A blessing . . . to East Texas and its children yet unborn." Sam Rayburn Reservoir stretches across what was once the Angelina bottom. Photo by Carolyn Chambliss.

with surprisingly little acrimony since. In any human endeavor, especially one involving opportunities for riches as vast as this one, you'd expect foul play. Yet the presence of Rayburn has been orderly, casting its fortunes fairly upon the great and small.

The waters of the Angelina River were dammed, spread out over freshly cut forests, drowned field and farm, rose steadily, and as an act of man and God, the rising of Rayburn was like a new day rising over East Texas. No one, not even LBJ or Mr. Sam himself, could have, in their fondest dreams, forecast what a blessing Lake Sam Rayburn would be to East Texas and its children yet unborn.

In 1993 I drove with my father toward Bevilport, a long-extinct riverboat landing on the Angelina River ten miles below Rayburn Dam. The road climbed over gentle hills and passed modest frame houses set here and there in cutover forests. Though I had ridden the school bus along this road daily in the 1950s, only occasionally did I now see a familiar house, a recognizable patch of woods. All had changed.

"This is Jack Brooks's land here along the road," Boose said with a wave of his hand. "It's a big place, and he owns a lot more than this.

"When he first went to Washington," he went on after a pause, "he didn't have a shittin' thing. Now he's a millionaire several times over."

The talk went to politicians and how they seemed to have lost touch with the people they were supposed to represent. We talked about Brooks and the building of the Rayburn Dam and Reservoir.

"Old LBJ never used that podium I built," Boose said. "Maybe Jack Brooks used it. We didn't go to the dedication."

After a pause he continued, "I never did know what happened to it. Last year Versie saw a stand down at the Corps of Engineers at the dam and thought it might be the one I built, but it wasn't."

At my question, he answered, "No, it wasn't very fancy. The Corps didn't think that was necessary. I made it out of plywood."

After a longer silence he laughed briefly, abruptly, as he often did to signal that a statement he was about to make had little consequence.

"I guess it would have been a good thing for people in the family to look back later and say their great-granddaddy built a speaker's stand for a president," he said.

18 The End of the River

In Xanadu did Kubla Khan
A stately pleasure dome decree:
Where Alph, the sacred river, ran
Through caverns measureless to man
  Down to a sunless sea.
Samuel Taylor Coleridge, "Kubla Khan"

If you look at a map of northern Jasper County made before the dam went in, you can see where the Angelina River entered a great bend about five miles south of the county line. The bend looks remarkably like a three-mile-high horse's head facing eastward. Several creeks coming from the east and southeast run into the horse's face — Beef Creek enters at the forelock, Hog Creek and Willow Branch halfway down the nose, and Mill Creek at the nostrils.

Corbett's hogs roamed the country bordered on the south by Mill Creek, on the north by Beef Creek, and on the west by the Angelina River. He could find hogs with his mark in their ears all the way to the headwaters of Hog Creek and beyond. Not a soul lived in this twenty-mile-square piece of country in the 1950s and 1960s; remoteness from a town and the infertility of pinewoods sand had driven the few original settlers out. Pa Graham's place at the southern end marked the last family farm to be occupied.

We hunted the uplands and camped and fished along the river from the horse's forehead to the tip of its nose. Lumber companies owned most of the bottomland and the adjacent uplands, but in those days their land stayed open to the public. Small patches of higher elevation bottomland along the river had been settled early on for farming but had long since been abandoned. Beyond the main woods roads, you seldom saw a person.

The old Warner place where Willow Branch and Hog Creek ran into the river remained the favorite campsite of my brother and me, and sometimes friends, during our teenage years. G. W. Warner and his wife, Katherine, had lived there and farmed the bottomland field until the need of schooling for their children had pulled them out of the bottom and into the Peachtree community. Loblolly pine saplings had invaded the higher and drier parts of the old field by the time we began camping in and near the small pine-board house they had left behind.

Here, with a shelter handy in case it rained, we passed weekends and vacations. Spring intoxicated you on the five-mile walk in, and the blooming of the dogwoods, azaleas, and grancy-gray-beard trees told you it was time for fish to bite. Summers we lounged on snow-white sandbars cleaned annually by floods; we searched the sandy bottom of the river with our toes to find the river mussels. From October through December the bottom hardwoods wore a coat of many changing colors, and we shot gray and fox squirrels and smoked the meat inside a tumbled building with a cypress shingle roof that once had sheltered chickens.

In low spots in the bottom, mud stains marked the oak and hickory trunks as high as you could reach and higher. When the river rose from rains, it spread out through the bottom, filling sloughs and potholes. Wood ducks flushed from these in winter. Once I shot a monster writhing in a swarm of tiny fish in a dark and log-filled pool, and when it floated lifeless to the surface, it turned into a two-foot grinnel, a fish I later heard called bowfin. It herds its young and takes them in its mouth in case of danger, say the books on fishes.

Over large expanses of the bottom woods, you could see a slough-edge heron or an armadillo fifty or a hundred yards in front of you. The hardwoods interlaced their branches overhead, shading out underbrush. Water during flood time helped by drowning some kinds

Angelina near the mouth of Hog Creek in the late 1950s, shortly before Rayburn Dam several miles upstream blocked the flooding.

of trees as seedlings. You could race along unhindered to chase a gray squirrel traveling tree-branch runways fifty feet above your head on its way to a hollow tree.

In winter, hogs loved to lie on the high places in these bottoms. Here, safe from all but major floods, they found occasional loblolly pines and rooted piles of needles into communal beds. Downwind from these places, you could smell the musky odor unlike anything but hog.

On spring and summer nights the barred owls rolled their ghostly calls up and down the river. Bullfrog and raccoon eyes flashed from riverbanks swept by flashlight, and flying squirrels coasted overhead from tree to tree.

Daytime dawning echoed to the call of pileated woodpeckers and a score or more of other kinds of birds. The sounds of squirrels chattering in the distance made your heart thump harder. Once I watched a mink patrol a slough bank on a misty morning.

We called this section of the Angelina simply the river. "Going to the river" meant walking north and west from home, or sometimes driving if drier weather made the roads passable, to reach the Angelina somewhere on the horse's face.

The farthest north along the river that I had walked from home had a tall hill near the river channel. To reach the hill you had to wade the wide and sandy-bottomed Beef Creek just above its mouth. Corbett called the curve of river near the hill McGee Bend, after an early family that had settled where the highlands met the bottom.

Then came that day in 1955 when I heard Corbett say to Fannie, "I hear they plan to build a dam up on the river. It's supposed to be at McGee Bend."

To Corbett, Fannie, and me, "they" signified an anonymous authority beyond our control. Only later did I learn that "they" in this case was the Fort Worth District of the U.S. Army Corps of Engineers.

I worried a little at the time but not a lot. McGee Bend seemed far enough outside my favorite haunts along the river that the building of a dam probably would not bring a lot of people to the woods or make much difference to the fishing. Shoot, you probably wouldn't even notice.

Next winter, when I heard they'd started work, I took another day-long walk to McGee Bend. I heard the revving of the Caterpillars by the time I crossed Beef Creek. From the hilltop on the other side I could see past leafless trees. The tractors looked like toys in the distant clearing, playing in a yellow gash of earth.

A brochure put together later by the U.S. Army Corps of Engineers said:

> When construction of the dam in the piney woods area of East Texas began in 1956, the project was known as "McGee Bend Dam and Reservoir." It was designed to control floods, generate hydro-electric power, and conserve water for municipal, industrial, agricultural, and recreational uses.

Project engineers took advantage of the great horsehead bend in the river. The dam when finished blocked the river at McGee Bend and shunted water to a spillway in the dam a mile or more to the west. From the spillway, water plunged into a channel cut across the horse's neck. The crafty engineers had bypassed the ten miles or so of river that had formed the horse's head, gaining several feet of drop from the surface of the reservoir to the pool below the spillway and thus a few more kilowatts of power from the generators.

The Corps of Engineers brochure said:

> In 1967 the Fort Worth District, Corps of Engineers, was awarded the Chief of Engineers' Outstanding Engineering Achievement Award for the design and construction of the powerhouse and outlet works.

Once the levee had been built, our stretch of the river turned into a long and shallow lake. Fed at the upper end only by Beef Creek and farther down by Hog Creek and Willow Branch, its rises and current almost stopped. During peak discharge from the dam's spillway, it rose a few feet — from the water backing upstream — and when Beef Creek rose from heavy rains you could sometimes see a little current just below the creek's mouth, but for all our purposes the river was no more.

By this time I had gone away to school, and it was through vacation's periodic window that I saw the river change. Bars of sand that had whitened every bend and crook turned to brush and briar tangles. Turtles found no sandy banks on which to lay their eggs, and the river channel clogged with mud that settled from the sluggish water. Fishing was no use; the scarcity of heron and raccoon tracks tried to tell me that before I sat all day without a bite.

The bottomlands dried out. Sloughs shrank to wrinkled mud and skeletons of turtles. Trucks found travel easier in the bottoms, and loggers hauled the bigger trees away. Wind carried loblolly seeds from the occasional pine in the bottomland to all the empty places, and their seedlings in remarkably short order cut the distance you could see in half, and then in half again. Shrubs and hardwood trees intolerant of flooding sprouted up and fought with pines to claim the openings.

One vacation I decided to visit Hole-in-the-Rock again, just beyond the river bottom's edge. I'd not been to it in several years but felt an urge to find a sanctuary from the changes. On the way in, I could see that even upland woods had been invaded. Fresh-cut stumps of pines and ruts of logging trucks lay at every hand; I barely recognized the Hog Creek bottomland for all the slash and almost never found the mound of rock.

Finally, the monolith loomed among the trees. When I drew near, I saw a heap of earth and rocks piled near the opening of the little cave. Someone had come with pick and shovel and had excavated it.

What had they sought? Around the small clearing the woods seemed suddenly two dimensional, just broken trees on a postcard. I never went back.

Shortly after that, I saw a clipping Versie had saved from the July 28, 1966, issue of the *Jasper News-Boy*. A photograph of Corbett's Old Wash Hole on Hog Creek, the holy ground of my youth, splashed across the page. Little-known secret of Jasper County, the paper said. Here's how to find it.

The Angelina River still flows the twenty miles or so between the dam and the river's confluence with the Neches. But, as the Corps of Engineers intended, it no longer floods high anywhere along this stretch or gets as low as it once did. It falls and rises with the rate of discharge through the spillway but never crests the brush-choked riverbanks to spill out to the flats beyond. If it did, the new homes that stand beside the river and that rim the oxbow lakes would get wet.

Now when you cross the river on Highway 63 below the dam, the water nearly always flows dark and clear beneath the bridge. Even when the level rises, mud no longer stains it brown, except on rare occasions when the flooding Neches backs its water upstream from where the Angelina joins it down below. The fertile silt that once in floodtime fed the trees and animals in the bottomland now settles out in the upper reaches of the reservoir.

The Corps of Engineers brochure tells us that politicians changed the project's name in 1963. People stopped calling it McGee Bend and began to speak of Sam Rayburn Dam and Reservoir. Mr. Sam's pork. The Eighty-eighth Congress of the United States legislated the change, in honor of "the late House Speaker Sam Rayburn, a champion of soil and water conservation."

When the river's current flows its swiftest past the Highway 63 bridge and the water nears the level of the boat docks on the bank, the local people say, "They're generatin'."

Above the dam, the reservoir swallows up fifty crow-flight miles of river and its bottomland. The length of streambed covered is perhaps a hundred miles, because beneath the lake the old river channel snakes back and forth. A map of Texas shows the lake to cover half of the original length of the Angelina River.

The reservoir contains a storage capacity of four million acre-feet of water, says the Corps of Engineers brochure. An acre-foot of water is one acre, one foot deep. When full, the reservoir covers 143,000 acres, or 225 square miles, nearly one-fifth the area of Rhode Island. The makers of the brochure may have known that Texans love superlatives: Rayburn Reservoir is the largest man-made lake within the state, they wrote.

As the reservoir filled, the lower parts of the Plum Ridge farm that Corbett and Fannie had bought and worked in their early married years sank beneath the water. A Plum Ridge village sprouted up a mile directly south on another piece of Pleistocene river terrace. When the reservoir filled up, the water stopped at the edge of the new settlement.

Versie and Boose bought an acre of land in the new Plum Ridge. It bordered on the water of the lake. At first, they commuted from their Peachtree home fifteen miles away to spend time there on weekends. Later on, they built a house. At night from the back side of the yard, you can look across the water and see the lights of cars crossing Mr. Rayburn's dam.

The original owner of the site where the new Plum Ridge proliferated built a brick home with the money he had made from selling land. More people moved into the lakeside community, mostly older folks retired on pensions. Those who continued working in the city built cottages or hauled in mobile homes and came on weekends and holidays.

Just after dark one Wednesday night in early December of 1993, I strolled from the edge of Rayburn Lake through Plum Ridge toward the missionary Baptist church on the outskirts of the settlement. Along the way, mobile homes on blocks looked across the street at concrete aprons spread in front of pink brick walls. In one yard, blinking lights illuminated plastic Santas. "Holy Night" tinkled from an outdoor speaker.

The ancient pine-board house of the original owner stared darkly. It looked an embarrassed gray in the midst of lights and tinsel. On its porch, in the beam of a vapor lamp, furniture relaxed in accidental postures. The new house next door resembled a mortuary with wrought-iron posts white against the brick.

Two houses down, a dozen golf carts lined a drive. Plum Ridge is ten miles from the nearest course or putting green; perhaps the golf cart salesman hoped to convince those reluctant to buy that even trailer occupants could purchase status. Cart ownership guaranteed one a slot in the Plum Ridge Fourth of July parade.

I heard automobile engines crank up, one here, another there. Headlights moved up the street the two hundred yards to the church. Cars and trucks converged beneath yet another vapor light in the balmy evening; people entered to an organ playing "It Came upon a Midnight Clear."

A few days later my mother took me to Corbett and Fannie's old homeplace where she had lived her early years. To get there, we climbed the hill beyond the church, turned right where the pavement met a sandy road, then a quarter mile beyond turned back toward the lake where a pile of trimmings from a Plum Ridge yard hid the entrance to a two-rut road.

We wound a mile or so downhill among longleaf pines. Suddenly the road leveled out, turned left, and shot straight across the flat beneath overhanging trees. A quarter mile later, it fell through a clay red slot off the table's edge and ended at a sandy beach beside the water.

"Daddy had his cornfield on this flat," my mother said. "He worked about twenty acres here with Old Queenie."

Loblolly pines towered overhead, the biggest ones a foot thick at the base. Here and there, sweetgum and blackgum trees fought to reach the sun, and yellow jessamine vines clung to yaupon, dogwood, and blueberry beneath the canopy of pine and gum. Cornfields could be seen only in memory.

"Right down there," she pointed into the lake, "stood the old church and the canning plant. The government built the canning factory in the early thirties, as I recall, to give the Plum Ridge people a place to put up food. A grove of holly trees where I used to play stood over there, and down beyond that in the bottom Daddy planted sugarcane and sometimes cotton."

We left the road fifty paces from the water's edge and fought our way through vines and briars to the old homesite. Secure once from river floods and now from Rayburn Lake, it perched on the flatland's edge, and from the tumbled sandstone chimney you could see the water glimmer through the bushes.

"Here's the well we used," Versie said as she pointed out a brick-lined hole nearly filled with dirt and leaves. "And Mama had the garden here. She grew everything, even some of that kohlrabi, which I haven't seen much of since. The garden gate hung here, beneath this old pecan."

I saw a rusty hinge nailed to a sagging board. The board and hinge clung to a post. With my pocketknife I cut into the post; the orange-yellow wood smelled of longleaf heart. I pushed against it, and it did not budge. It had stood there sixty years, with still no sign of rot.

My mother looked beyond the homesite and through the trees, maybe thinking of a cornfield and Corbett plowing with Old Queenie.

"Every winter late when the corn got low in the crib," she said, "the rats didn't have any place to hide, and we'd have a rat killing. One time the county commissioner came by when we were chasing the rats out of the last of the corn. He had on a pair of high-top leather boots, I guess to protect his legs, but when a rat ran up his boot, he really done a jig."

As we left the old homestead and climbed the hill, she said, "Daddy had his cows out in the piney woods. He'd take a little corn out on the highest hill and call and they would come.

"When Kirby's people cut the timber in the early thirties, they left hardly any trees on these hills," she continued. "It was all grass.

"Not long after that, we moved to Peachtree. But Mama loved it here. She didn't want to leave."

Now the roar of motors splits the weekend air, and the thump-thump-thump of speedboats slapping waves helps justify the dam. An open sheet of water has replaced the land and all its hidden corners. No longer do the people mingle with the plants and animals in the landscape; they ride across the water and sometimes drop a lure where their depth-finder signifies a likely spot for bass.

But nearly everybody seems to like the new way. In boats they ply the lake, and from Winnebagos and trailers at its margin they plug into power outlets. Nearby in the National Forest land surrounding

The end of the river. The Corps of Engineers cut and scraped and molded, and the
Sam Rayburn Dam and Reservoir took form where the Angelina used to run.
Photo by Carolyn Chambliss.

Plum Ridge, a day's walk through the woods can be a lonely one; the only signs of human presence off the roads are the rutted trails blazed by four-wheeled Hondas that are piloted by plastic-coated kids from town.

People seem to have become addicted to the power of machines. Their presence is announced by the noise of a gasoline motor, an air conditioner, or a television set. Only on occasion can one see an old man with a paddle maneuvering his boat among the lake-edge snags, and sometimes in the evening shadows, an aging couple walks the road that climbs the hill beyond the church.

19 Corporate State

O! how wretched is that poor man that hangs on princes' favors!
William Shakespeare, Henry VIII

In the mid-1980s my brother, Jack, built a house. During its construction I drove out to pay a visit. From Plum Ridge at the margin of Sam Rayburn Lake, the way to Jack's led south, holding to the high ground between the Neches and the Angelina Rivers and heading for their confluence.

Nearing Jack's eight acres, I swung sharply left where the gravestones of a cemetery stood at attention in a grassy opening on the right. Red oak, loblolly pine, and hickory trees edged against the road. On my Jasper County map the cemetery looked to be about three miles east of the Neches, three miles west of the Angelina, and three or four miles north of Bee Tree Slough, that swamp and bayou land known as Forks of the River. I heard the chain saw as I pulled into the drive.

Sawdust peppered Jack's hair and beard where he straddled a loblolly log. He switched the chain saw off.

"Howdy," he said. "Get out and come in."

There was not a house to "come in" to, but a new-cut framework stark against the green of trees spoke of one to come. Jack lit a cigarette. The rosin smell of pine mingled with the scent of smoke. He found a place free of pitch and sat down on the log.

"What are you doing?" I asked, eyeing the lengthwise cut in the foot-thick log, a slit that ran straight down the middle and halfway to completion. Blocks of wood held the log several inches off the ground.

"Making lumber," he said, pulling on the cigarette.

Smoke erupted from his nose, and I waited for a further explanation. None came.

"How?" I finally asked.

"With this chain saw," he replied, wrinkling his face into a halfway smile that showed the gap in front where he had lost a lower tooth in a motorcycle accident.

The cigarette had dwindled to a half-inch stub when he dropped it to the ground. He twisted the butt into the leaves with his boot. He lifted the chain saw by the grip with his left hand and yanked it into life with his right, careful to keep the bar and chain some distance from his thigh.

"You cut the log right down the middle at first," he spoke loudly to be heard over the putter of the saw. "Like this."

He revved the motor up and eased the whirring chain into the slit. Sawdust spurted out. He rocked the saw back and forth, and hungrily it ate its way down the log. When it reached the end, the two halves of the log fell apart and showed a straight, even cut down the eight-foot length.

Then, with half of the log braced to keep the first cut vertical, Jack began another cut about an inch apart from the first. The saw moved down the log again.

"I heard you could get a chain saw guide to keep the cuts straight and the thickness of the boards uniform," he said, raising up to rest. "But after a little practice, it looked like I didn't need one."

Ten minutes later, when the new-made board fell from the now-diminished half log, I lifted it to eyeball down its length and feel its thickness. I agreed with Jack's assessment.

"Here, let me show you how the house is coming," he said.

The framework sat on concrete posts sunk into the ground and standing two feet high. Jack had poured the concrete into molds made of gallon coffee cans with both ends cut out and the cans stacked end to end. All the boards looked like chain-sawed lumber — the sills that sat atop the concrete posts, the floor joists nailed edgewise on the tops of sills, the flooring, and the wall studs just now rising.

"There was plenty of loblolly pine amongst the hardwoods on this land," Jack said, showing me where he had cut the trees to get the lumber. "It didn't take as many trees as I first thought it would. I just used it green, and it's drying in place. The boards will shrink some, so I guess I'll have to add another layer of flooring later and use batts to cover up the cracks between the siding boards."

"Why didn't you just go down to the lumberyard or sawmill and buy the lumber?" I asked.

"Well," he said, "it's partly a matter of principle. I got to thinking about the taxes taken from my paycheck, and all the politicians and other unproductive people those taxes help support. And then there's the sales tax on top of that."

He turned and started back toward his partly sawed log.

"This way, I won't help support those public welfare programs I don't agree with." Jack laughed. "Besides, it's kind of fun. Maybe the McCullough company would pay me for a story about building a house with one of their saws."

Jack went back to work, and I walked around his property. Stumps dotted a first-year garden plot. Cardinals moved into and out of the yaupon undergrowth that edged the clearing. The swishing of a hickory branch beyond showed a gray squirrel move away.

Jack valued his independence. I thought about the pros and cons of his approach to house building. I could see two economic disadvantages. First, Jack's monetary return for his effort might have been better if he had worked the same hours earning a reasonable wage from a business and had bought the lumber. Second, the appearance of the house when finished would not match that of the "proper" house as built by a contractor and shown in ads, and this might shrink its appeal to a TV-conditioned buyer should Jack decide to sell.

The advantages could not be measured quite as easily but might have been a good deal more important. The first and second Jack himself had noted: he controlled who benefitted from his efforts, and he felt good about his work. I could see others. By keeping a measure of economic independence from employer and government, he stayed closer to the ages-old security of self-reliance. He knew his house; it was part of him, and it was strong. He could see the impacts of his actions on the land and change them if he wished. He could speak his mind independently of corporate oversight and political correctness.

Later, when the house acquired walls, a roof, doors, and electricity, Jack's wife, Darlene, and daughter, Kathy, came. The next summer the garden grew in size and in variety of crops—black-eyed peas, okra, Irish and sweet potatoes, corn, squash, beans, and melons. Chickens cackled from the barn. Darlene canned food and put up vegetables. One day in fall when hunting season opened, Kathy climbed up to a platform Jack had built in the hickory tree behind their house and shot a deer to add to their store of food. In winter they warmed the house with wood cut just beyond the garden.

With part-time jobs now, they buy the manufactured things that make life easier or more entertaining. One of these is a television, and from my visits I know they watch the evening news. Perhaps they wonder at the desperation in the eyes of laid-off workers in the streets of Houston. Almost certainly they pay scant attention to the cries of labor unions startled by the sound of jobs rushing south to Mexico. Corbett would have been pleased.

In 1967 the respected Harvard economist John Kenneth Galbraith published a book entitled *The New Industrial State*. In this book he voiced a concern about America's industrialized society: ". . . we are becoming the servants in thought, as in action, of the machine we have created to serve us." His analysis echoed the theme that Aldous Huxley's *Brave New World* had satirically proposed thirty-five years earlier.

This idea might have seemed foolish to most. In a single generation Americans had witnessed the explosion of benefits generated by the corporate state. Industrial growth following World War II had paralleled an unprecedented economic boom. By the 1950s the industrial machine under corporate management could produce much more than people were buying—by 1955 the average American had about five times as many dollars to spend after taking care of his basic needs as he had had in 1940.

Social critic Vance Packard believed this surplus of available money led corporations to step up their advertising. Advertising is good, they told each other. It makes volume selling easier and thus cuts down on the unit cost of items. The corporations hired professional psychoanalysts from universities to train their advertising staffs to stimulate people to buy their products, and so-called motivational research blossomed.

Advertisers emphasized the status that their products could bring. Television, which became available to Americans in the 1940s, proved to be the perfect medium for advertising. In 1950 less than 10 percent of Americans owned sets, but by 1960 nearly all homes had a TV—more houses had televisions than had indoor plumbing. TV claimed a captive audience in America's living rooms. As with other businesses, TV networks soon belonged to major corporations. The "consumer generation" had come of age.

Don't question prosperity, enjoy it, said the people by their actions. Galbraith's book received acclaim among some academic types, but few of the newly affluent even knew it existed.

Corbett and Fannie didn't read Galbraith's kind of book, but neither did they subscribe to foolish buying. I never saw them turn on the television they purchased in the early sixties, though I suppose they watched it on occasion. Never go to the store for what you can grow or shoot, I learned from them and my parents. Only those corporations that made shoes, household appliances, and substitutes for horses benefitted much from Fannie's hard-earned hog money.

I didn't know what Corbett thought about his brothers moving to jobs in town. They undoubtedly made more money than he did; I remember seeing a great chandelier hanging in the living room of one of them and wondering why we weren't allowed to play there. They got nearly all their food from stores, I guess, though Corbett always saved some pork for his favorite brother, Ragan.

I have always been glad that Corbett stayed in Peachtree. Life might have been less exciting for me had he moved to town. Much later, I began to understand the economic pressures that had lured his brothers away.

The substitution of machines for human labor had pushed people off the farm and into town beginning with the earliest days of the industrial revolution. The twentieth century came, and corporations teamed with trucks and tractors to accelerate this trend, sending family farmers to the city and corporate ownership to farms. Back in 1800, when self-sufficiency was common in America, only 5 percent of the people lived in urban areas, but by 1990 more than 75 percent lived in cities larger than fifty thousand people. Nearly all Americans had stopped producing food.

Today, less than 1 percent of the nation's workers farm. Two million people, mostly corporate employees, feed 250 million.

One reason for this trend is that the corporate farmer produces and delivers food more cost-effectively than the family farmer. For example, since 1940 when the escalating corporate takeover of farming foretold a continuing trend, American farmers have doubled crop production, without much increase in the total acreage farmed. The average size of each farm, however, has grown to fit the pocketbooks of corporations and the costs of diesel tractors spanning several rows of corn.

The dependence of American farmers on petroleum — the game that Corbett ventured into when he bought his tractor — has become so nearly complete that feeding the nation without a steady oil supply is now impossible. Fertilizer and pesticide production drink oil almost as thirstily as the trucks and trains that take the food from farms to town and haul the fuel and fertilizer from town to farm.

At the same time that oil has cut the dollar cost of food production, it has upped the energy cost tremendously. Food production experts calculate that farming at subsistence levels, as Corbett's family did before the Model T and tractor, requires about one unit of human or animal energy to produce ten units of food energy. Modern farming, on the other hand, uses ten units of energy, mainly from oil, to produce and deliver one unit of food energy. That's a hundredfold increase since Corbett's youth in the energy needed to fill a dinner plate.

We are caught in an energy trap. We can't move en masse back to the farm, to till the land by hand; our industrialized system needs us to work in town. Such a move would send both food and factory production plummeting, rousing the specter of economic collapse. So we'll probably continue to squirm, however uncomfortably, where we are, riding on the coattails of the corporation. And hope the oil keeps flowing.

On March 29, 1994, Jim Barlow, columnist for the business section of the *Houston Chronicle*, lamented the preparations of his neighbor to move to the East Coast. The man worked as an engineer. His employer, a major corporation, had undergone a "restructuring."

Barlow used the incident to comment on the changing American corporation. Expect more of this, he said. The world has changed. Beginning in the late 1940s, we sought our fortunes in large organizations; they welcomed us as family. They guaranteed security from puberty to grave.

The organization family is no more. Children and grandparents of the work force find themselves turned out on the street. To stay viable the company must cut back its payroll, go high tech, adjust its practices. To stay employed the worker must retrain, move, or find another job — or all three.

My neighbor doesn't qualify as a "victim" of restructuring, Barlow concluded. He's just working for a company that's trying to stay viable.

Like Jim Barlow's neighbor, most corporate workers live in cities. Many accept moving from town to town as part of the job. Uniformity among the cities of America has made the necessary moving easier. Familiar-looking city parks, shopping malls, and programs on the television set are always standing by to make the migrant feel at home. No longer do displaced people have to face the absolute strangeness of an unfamiliar landscape.

But the corporate gypsy faces hidden risks. Traditions that for generations told people how to get their sustenance from land become lost. Few in cities have the space even to grow a garden. With the loss of self-reliance comes the loss of independence. Corporate workers have come far toward fulfilling John Kenneth Galbraith's prophecy: we have become the servants of the machines we created to serve us.

The sun had barely topped the trees on a spring day in 1994 when Dan Lay and I climbed into the cab of Bob Little's pickup on the outskirts of Nacogdoches in the upper Angelina valley. Bob had promised to show us a modern logging operation. He managed timber harvesting for Louisiana-Pacific, or simply L-P, which older people would know as a timber company. Bob calls L-P's business "wood products" to reflect the company's wider interests — from the cutting of a tree to its transformation into paper and houses.

"I think we'll go out east of town a ways," he said, his "out" sounding to an ear trained in Texas like "boot" without the "b." "I should be able to show you some equipment at work on one of our cuts."

Bob Little took to forestry because he loved being in the woods.

"In western Virginia where I grew up," he said, "I liked to climb up the mountain to a hickory grove and wait for squirrels."

We drove several miles of paved road and continued beyond where it yielded to bumpy dirt. Bob talked of economics and the harvesting of wood.

"Profit is the bottom line," he said. "We have to stay competitive or fold. L-P does try to keep within what the forest industry calls 'best management practices' as far as conserving wildlife habitat or preventing soil erosion or water pollution. Though we don't always have control over our loggers, who work under contract to us, we sometimes give preference to logging contractors with modern machinery because their operations tend to cause less erosion and other undesirable side effects.

"To substitute machines for human labor saves money for the logging contractor," he continued. "L-P has found this also to be the case in our own operations. With the increasing costs of employee insurance, unemployment checks, and other worker benefits, it just makes sense to go high tech and maintain smaller payrolls."

Bob slowed the truck as we approached a rutted turnoff. He pulled onto the side road, and we entered a woods of mostly small loblolly and shortleaf pine trees interspersed with sweetgum, red oak, and other hardwoods. Treetops and severed branches littered the ground.

"Looks like they've got a shear going," Bob said as he pointed to a resin-dotted stump projecting just a few inches above the leaves on the forest floor.

We topped a rise, and diesel engines sounded in the distance. Bob steered the truck along the new-made road, slowing where the ruts had sunk in softer ground. Movement showed itself beyond a screen of trees as the pickup lurched sharply from the ruts and stopped beneath a hickory tree.

Logging operations charged the air with the sounds and smells of harvest. As Bob killed the engine, we heard cracking branches and the thump of trees crashing to the ground. The odor of hardwood sap and upturned soil, tainted with the fragrance of resin from fresh-cut pine trees, engulfed us as we climbed down from the truck.

The growling of the diesel engines rose a notch in amplitude. Bob led us up a slope toward the sound. Then he stopped, and we beheld an awesome sight. Surging down the hill in our direction came a dingy yellow monster behind gleaming jaws. It bent at midsection to twist its way among tree trunks. Seemingly driverless, it climbed over logs with its four balloon tires churning. As it moved, it changed direction sharply and unpredictably.

Bob strode ahead, and I felt the urge to shout a warning as the machine approached him. *Star Wars* images of pincers reaching for helpless victims momentarily replaced reality. Bob seem unperturbed.

Suddenly the looming shape made a right-angle turn. Catlike, it lunged for a pine tree, snapping its jaws like a three-fingered hand around the trunk. A whirring saw blade slid in just above ground level. Its whispering dropped to a low groan, and shavings spurted to the side.

One, two, three seconds and the two-foot-thick pine tree leaned and rose slightly from the ground. The claw lifted the severed body and, with a snap, bent it like a limber switch and smashed it to the ground. Branches cracked and leaves boiled up. Instantly the machine loosed its hold and changed directions, lunging now toward Bob to sever another tree and whip it downward as if in threat. Still Bob made no move, and soon it backed away and moved over the hill out of sight.

"Saw-head shear," Bob explained as I moved toward him, nonchalantly I hoped. "Four-wheel drive and eight tons or so of weight. You want to be careful not to get too close because sometimes a really big tree will flip the machine."

Something moved in the woods to the left of where the shear had disappeared. Down the hill rolled a John Deere tractor, dragging several logs bunched with their butt ends lifted off the ground by a claw dangling from a steel frame on the tractor's posterior. Corbett would have marveled at the size and agility of this modern cousin of his 1940s two-cylinder machine. The sound of its diesel motor muffled the scraping of the logs on the ground.

"Most logging contractors now use skidders similar to this," said Bob. "They are a lot more efficient than the old practice of dragging logs out one at a time. Also, by keeping the forward ends of the logs from gouging into the ground, the skidders cut down on trenching and erosion."

An empty log truck crept past on the road by which we had entered, the single pipe that comprised most of its length folded like a grasshopper's leg and its rear wheels carried piggyback. It turned around in a small opening at the end of the road where the skidder had built a pile of logs. Its load of wheels dropped to the ground, and the jointed pipe extended itself slowly, pushing the wheels backward from the cab. Soon the long arm of the loader began stacking logs between the uprights of the extended bed.

"These log trucks are similar to what's been used for years," said Bob, "but this shear and another machine we call a de-limber are pretty new technology. The de-limber is best for use on plantations where tree size and spacing is uniform; it cuts the tree and also trims the limbs and cuts the log to length. Logging operations are going more and more mechanical because it's economically more efficient."

The human "de-limbers" for this operation soon moved in with their chain saws, trimming branches from the fallen trees and cutting trunks to prescribed lengths. Muscled and remarkably swift, the sawyers angled their saws ahead of them as they strode beside the logs. They scarcely paused, and the limbs on the prostrate trees fell like dominoes. Their saws kept up a steady, pumping rhythm — zing-zing-zing — like a tiny motorcycle engine being revved in preparation for a wheelie. They stopped to talk.

These flatheads, as people sometimes called sawyers even now, wore leggings of a coarse-grained weave. The chaps of one man in particular showed signs of frequent contact with the saw.

"No, I don't believe this material is the same stuff that's used for making bullet-proof vests," he laughed in answer to a question. "But it does help keep the saw chain off your leg."

How soon would the jobs of these men give way to de-limbers built to harvest weedy stands? We have to remain competitive, said Bob.

The chain saw men went back to work, and we went back to the truck parked beneath the hickory tree.

"So far, on its own lands L-P has stayed away from clear-cutting and putting in pine plantations," Bob said. "It's been cheaper for us to just thin stands and let natural tree reproduction take its course. Logging like you see here prepares a seedbed by its nature; it stirs up the soil surface.

"Other companies might be moving toward our selective-cutting practice. It's hard to tell. Plantations have some economic disadvantages. For example, southern pine beetles spread more rapidly in pure pine stands than they do when hardwoods are mixed in, mainly because the pines are packed closely together. Some foresters now report seeing even very young trees on plantations killed by beetles, which hasn't been a common thing before.

"Of course, we're now beginning to plant hardwoods on some sites that are wet or otherwise unsuited to pines. In bottomlands, for example. Shumard oak is one of the species used. The price for hardwood pulp for making top grades of paper has gone up, so hardwood plantations look more attractive to our managers than before. Hardwoods may soon be more valuable than pine, as they were earlier in this century."

I looked up at the bare branches spreading over the truck. The bark looked like that of the mockernut. Cautious like other hickories, the tree would wait until all danger of frost had passed to put out leaves. Remnants of a few nuts from the year before lay among the dead leaves on the ground.

"This tree has no more value to us than any other hardwood — oak, gum, or even cottonwood," Bob said. "In fact, the bigger ones like this are hard to handle with our machines. I've made it a practice to leave large hickories and oaks when we can; cutting them offers little economic incentive, and they're good for wildlife.

"L-P has its own nursery for producing hardwood seedlings," he went on. "We grow quite a few species, most of which we give away to others for landscaping, reclaiming disturbed sites, and so on. It's good publicity. More and more landowners seem interested in managing for wildlife and plant diversity."

On our way back to town, Bob talked about the future of the private forests. What happens depends mainly on what makes the most economic sense, he reminded us. That's how a timber products company stays afloat.

"One of the reasons conversion of mixed stands of timber to single-species pine plantations has been so popular is that it's been subsidized," he said. "And it still is. The Texas Forestry Association, comprised of timber companies and other landowners in the state, often pays a majority of the cost for pine plantings. Not only that, they also help pay the costs of killing hardwoods."

"I've seen plantations subsidized for many years," broke in Dan. "Federal agencies such as the Soil Conservation Service and the Agricultural Stabilization and Conservation Service have provided taxpayers' money to help landowners convert hardwood stands to pine plantations."

"Pine plantations, if properly managed, produce more wood fiber than natural stands," Bob said by way of explaining one rationale for these subsidies. "A good tree farmer selects not only the species best suited for his soils and region but also a genetic stock known to grow faster. By planting at high densities, he can shade out competing species that tend to naturally invade. Using mechanical harvesters allows him to thin stands efficiently at given tree ages, maintaining maximum rates of tree growth."

It made sense. Modern farmers of other kinds also selected their plant varieties with care, kept out competing weeds, and thinned and harvested on particular schedules to get highest yields. But such intensive management required subsidies of energy, and the affordable level of care depended on the price of the energy and the demand for the farm product.

"Demand for wood products varies over time," said Bob, "and the relative profitability of each management practice changes. That's why we have to keep a close eye on the markets and on new products and technologies. That's why it's hard to predict exactly what we'll be doing in ten, twenty, or thirty years from now.

"Right now we're moving more and more toward OSB and LVL," he said. "It's economical for us.

"OSB means oriented strand board," Bob explained, "that is, sheets of lumber similar to plywood but made of glue and long wood chips. We make LVL, or laminated veneer lumber, by gluing strips of wood together. That way we can use small trees to make large structural timbers."

"Your company makes money from land in ways other than growing and harvesting trees, doesn't it?" asked Dan. "What about hunting leases?"

"All of the lands we own yield returns from hunting rights," replied

Bob. "L-P recently hired a wildlife biologist to advise us about managing wildlife and hunters. He recommends, for example, what kinds of plants — oats, wheat, and so on — we should sow to attract deer to hunting blinds. He also evaluates the effects of various timber management practices on wildlife. Other timber companies also are beginning to employ wildlife experts.

"Most of our fee lands are leased from us by private hunting clubs or by the state for hunting or fishing rights," he said. "Recently we've set aside a few tracts where our employees can hunt, as a sort of fringe benefit of employment."

"How much are hunting rights worth?" asked Dan.

"Oh, the hunting clubs pay about $2.50 per acre per year on up to $3.75 on the better hunting parcels. That's a modest income for L-P, nothing like the $50-plus per acre we get from timber on good sites.

"L-P is concerned about small game and songbirds as well as deer," Bob went on. "Public interest demands it." After a pause, he added, "The constant changes in the markets and in timber management practices present a real challenge to wildlife biologists."

Back in Nacogdoches, Bob talked more about his personal life. Like the wildlife on a tract of timberland, he feels more comfortable with a diversity of resources. In addition to his regular job, he invests in stocks. This may help him buy a better future for himself, his wife, and their two daughters. Sometimes he thinks he might have better followed a profession that offered greater economic opportunity than forestry.

Then perhaps he could have had the time and money to afford to spend more weekends in a special piece of woods. A place where he could wait for squirrels in a hickory grove.

Woe unto them that join house to house, that lay field to field, till there be no place, that they may be placed alone in the midst of the earth!

Isaiah 5:8

In science they teach you how to measure big things by taking small samples. Dipping your finger into the cake dough for a taste can tell you about the entire cake without your having to eat it all. That's sampling. Chemists measure quality in lakes by taking water samples. A day's swing through the Angelina woods in fall when I was young gave me a rough measure of squirrel abundance in a wider stretch of countryside. I called it hunting, but it also turned out to be a kind of sampling.

In 1994 I took a sample of the landscape in the Angelina country. It seemed to me that the woods had changed a lot, and I wanted to see how much. Boose drove the car along the road between the Peachtree place and Plum Ridge, and I watched beyond the roadsides on the left and right. A biologist might have called it taking a strip sample; Versie called it looking out the window. We started at Peachtree.

Close against the east side of the Peachtree place sits a remnant patch of hammock land — Ragan's woods. The timber has been high-graded, but hardwoods remain. Beneath the larger trees in Ragan's woods I see thickly growing cherry laurel, ironwood, yaupon, and greenbriar. Beech, magnolia, sugar maple, holly, and several kinds of hickories and oaks loom above. A big loblolly stands beside the dim roadbed on the lower end where seventy years ago John Kirby's tram-road and train pierced the stand and bared the ground to let the vagrant seed of pine take root.

Outside of Ragan's woods in all directions I see pine, pasture, and logging slash. An outsider taking stock of the surroundings might think Ragan's hardwood trees a curiosity and wonder how they got there. Only in a few other corners of East Texas are there remnant stands of oaks, maples, beech, and hickory.

Ragan's woods in 1994 are home for gray squirrels and several kinds of birds found nowhere else nearby. The hardwood trees feed and hide deer, raccoons, opossums, and other animals, some of which range also into adjoining places. In surrounding pasturelands and pinelands, the number of wild animals that are permanent residents approaches zero.

Leaving Ragan's woods and the pasture that surrounds the tumbling house I grew up in, we exit the gate beside Corbett's old homesite. Land recently stripped bare of all trees flanks us on both sides now. After we travel a mile or two past posted signs on right and left, we come to a place where the surface of the road shows more sand. A sign nailed to a tree beside the road proclaims: "Hog Creek Hunting Club."

Here, more than seventy-five years ago, pines grew mixed with hardwoods, and Kirby's lumbermen encountered fewer farms than at the Peachtree place. Timber companies own the land now, and its uniform appearance speaks of large individual parcels. Young loblolly pines ten to thirty feet tall crowd against each other and blanket the ground with fallen needles. Here and there, rotting hardwood trees cast their leafless bones against the sky; aerial spraying has selectively killed them.

Only club members have access to this land, and they hunt mainly for deer. Most animals are scarce in these kinds of woods. Deer multiplied at first when Caterpillars cleared the way for planting pines.

They've since declined as pines shaded out other plants. As the timber manager becomes yet more efficient at growing trees for wood, nearly all animals will have to look elsewhere.

An advertisement in a local paper says: "Temple-Inland's managed forests are yielding up to twice the wood volume per acre as unimproved pine stands. These productive forests mean that the wood and paper products Americans depend on will be provided for generations to come."

Shortly the road bumps perpendicularly into another. A right-hand turn would take us deeper among the juvenile pines and eventually to the Angelina River, if we could get past gates locked against nonmembers. The chances for this seem slim, so we turn left, and two miles later reach U.S. Highway 63. A right turn, and from here it's a straight shot to the Plum Ridge turnoff.

Soon beside Highway 63 we see a "River Ridge Hunting Club" sign on the right. The telltale hardwood snags overlook thickly growing loblolly pines a little older than those growing in the Hog Creek Hunting Club.

Half a mile before we reach the Angelina River bridge, we decide to make a quick diversion to the site of Old Zavala, where Isaac Graham settled down and Corbett lived his boyhood days. We turn right.

For two miles, a stand of twenty-foot loblolly pines restricts visibility to nearly zero on both sides of the road. Smaller stands of older loblolly and shortleaf pine rise up taller here and there. Dead oaks oversee the pine invasion. In an open spot a plywood deer blind painted green sits thirty feet above the ground on stilts — you can see the slot through which the hunters look for deer. Young pines sprouting in the clearing spell a short life for this deer-hunting place.

The road winds up a hill that overlooks the Angelina River and its bottomland, neither of which is visible because a crowding stand of loblollies and yaupons blocks the view. The narrow lane ends beside a cemetery. Pines that reach to eighty feet crowd against the fence. Among the graves a granite slab reaches to my chin. The chiseled letters read:

SITE OF THE TOWN OF ZAVALA
Established upon land included in the Empresario Grant in 1829 to Lorenzo De Zavala in whose honor it was named. Early boat

landing. Mail and stage station. Incorporated in 1838. A post office until the Civil War.

A lone magnolia spreads its branches wide above the graves as if to give those buried there a vestige of familiar habitat.

Back on Highway 63, we cross the Angelina, now confined within its banks by the Rayburn Dam and Reservoir upstream. An ancient cypress here and there rears its head above the dryland trees that are slowly closing in. Houses, all less than twenty-five years old, cluster on the riverbank.

A few miles later the bottom grades into hills, and the first longleaf pines appear, telling us that the soil is the poorest we have seen so far. The sign beside the highway identifies yet a different owner: "Angelina National Forest." Soon we slow down for the Plum Ridge turnoff.

The pavement narrows. The woodland opens up, and the blackened bases of the longleaf pine trees tell us why — employees of the U.S. Forest Service from time to time set fires to clear the underbrush. The longleaf trees stand tall and far apart, and in places we can see a hundred yards or more into the woods. A century ago we might have seen a turkey or a bear.

Longleaf pines live among a hundred other kinds of plants. They house a rare bird, the red-cockaded woodpecker, and feed with their seeds a range of animals from squirrels to turkeys. Their relatives, the loblollies, try to push out other kinds of living things and shed small, stingy seeds.

We near Sam Rayburn Reservoir. The road leads down the hill toward the Ice Age river terrace that holds the Plum Ridge settlement and flanks the lake. Blackjack oak, red oak, dogwood, and blueberry grow among the longleaf as we near the flat. To the left and right the land drops off into ravines among bay trees, beeches, hickories, and ironwood. As we leave the public forest and enter Plum Ridge, a gray squirrel and a pair of cardinals flit across the road to a rattan tangle. Behind them in a yard swings a front-porch feeding station.

In early March of 1994 I drove down from Plum Ridge to see Jack's wild hog. As I neared Jack's place, the woods opened to the left, and I could see the house on a rise beyond the pond. It had grown considerably from the frame of chain-sawed boards I remembered seeing as it first took shape, and its habitat had changed from woods to an open acreage dotted here and there with hickory, oak, and gum.

As I stopped the car, a low, wheeled movement swept from the garden toward me. It took on an identity: Kathy on the four-wheeler. From underneath the house bounced a wad of sticks and leaves stuck to Velcro. It was Fuzzybutt, the five-pound poodle, looking like an uptown boy gone bad.

Jack put down his hoe, and Darlene put the coffee on the stove. We sat beneath the budding dogwood by the steps and talked. Fuzzybutt decided he remembered me. A crow cawed.

"We had a box trap set by that low place over there," Jack responded to a question about the hog. He gestured with his hand. "Coons travel up and down that little creek. Kathy's caught quite a few.

"Anyway, one morning last week I went down to check the coon trap. Something had sprung it, and all the corn we used for bait was gone. The same something had squashed a plastic Pepsi bottle we'd partly filled with corn. I found hog tracks all around.

"We'd never seen a woods hog around here," he continued. "The tracks made me curious. So I made a trap with four-foot net wire and built a drop-door made of boards."

Darlene refilled our coffee cups. Jack lit a cigarette. He took a long draw and exhaled the smoke.

"Well, I caught a hog the first night," he said, watching the cigarette held between his fingers. "But it got out."

He took another pull on his cigarette. "The wire was bent down a little at the top of the trap. I guess he jumped over. So I added another two feet of height to the trap and angled the wire inward at the top."

Two crows searched the ground for food down by the pond. A flash of red advertised a cardinal in the yaupon bushes beyond the barn. Jack continued.

"The second night, I caught him," he said. "He's real wild, a boar. No marks in his ears; he's probably never been in a pen before.

"Do you want to see him?" he asked, flipping his cigarette butt to a grassy spot. "The trap's right down the hill by that baygall."

As we approached the trap, the hog stood unmoving on the far side. Black with a band of dingy white behind his shoulders, he looked small and lean in comparison with the fleshy giants at hog farms. He had a woods hog shape; where the classic pigs of children's books and butcher shops have tiny heads stuck like harmless afterthoughts on meaty bodies, the head of this hog dwarfed his frame, and the upper lips pooched outward where the tusks projected. Blood smeared his snout, and you could see the places in the netting where he had tried to root his way outside.

Suddenly he leaped. In a single bound, he cleared the eight-foot length of pen and halted only inches from the wire. He let loose a startling "woof," followed by a rapid snapping of the jaws at least as frightening as the burst of fire from an enemy's machine gun. I struggled to appear unruffled but felt my heart begin to pound.

Net wire made the trap's floor impervious to rooting. Jack pointed out the drop-door and the ingenious trigger he had made.

"I baited it with corn," he said.

The hog stood motionless in his new position. I leaned closer. His eyes changed from close-set beads of evil to orbs of liquid brown, fringed above by inch-long lashes. Unblinkingly alert and almost human, the eyes looked guarded. Only the trembling of his head and ears bespoke an inner turmoil, certainly not of fear, for he did not back away, but perhaps of longings seldom known to those of us who spend our lives in cages.

"I can't get him to eat or drink during the day," Jack said, pointing to the corn that littered the floor of the trap. "But next morning all the food and some of the water will be gone."

As we walked around the trap, the hog shifted positions so as to always face us. Tremors shook his ears from time to time. When someone neared the fence he leaped forward and popped his teeth together. I saw scarred, hairless patches on each side of his shoulders — from fighting other boars, Corbett would have said.

"I don't know where he came from," Jack said as we walked back toward the house. "I guess from the river bottom. It's not too far from here to the forks of the Angelina and the Neches, and that's still wild country. Maybe he came out to find food; we had a poor acorn crop last fall. Some of the 'coons we caught were real thin."

"When Jack built the trap," Darlene said later that evening, "I was hoping he would catch a sow and pigs. We could have fattened the young ones up, and they would be good eating. But I'm not sure about that old boar. I think Jack should turn him loose."

"People say the bad taste goes away if you castrate them," Jack responded. "I've heard it takes only a few months if they're well fed. We didn't get a deer this year and could use the meat."

In the evening silence, conversation died, and a baying of hounds sounded from the woods about half a mile away. I listened; the voices of the distant dogs rippled with excitement, silenced, then broke again into a babble. Curiously, they never changed direction, as is normal for a pack chasing quarry.

"Our neighbor chases foxes with his dogs," Darlene explained. "The reason they seem to not be going anywhere is that they're all in a pen. The man's built a fox-proof fence around his forty acres, turns a fox and hounds loose inside, and sits on his porch by the house listening to them run."

"I'm not sure what it's all for," commented Jack. "It's sort of like these baying pens that have gotten to be popular. You see them advertised in the local papers or on a sign beside the road. People take a mean hog, sort of like the one I caught, and put him in a pen with dogs. The dog that shows the most grit catching the hog by the ear and holding him, or just fighting him, wins."

The distant chase still sounded on the evening air when I left.

When I visited Jack again ten days later, he and Darlene's brother, Ernest, had "tended to" the boar. I saw the noose they had made of twisted nylon webbing; it hung from a rope that ran through a pulley suspended from a stout pole eight feet above the bottom of the trap.

"I climbed up above the pen on these poles," Jack said, "and finally managed to get the hog to walk through the noose. Then I drew it tight around his chest, and Ernest and I hoisted him up off the ground. We had a hell of a time lifting him; he's heavier than he looks. But once we got him to the top of the pen we tied the rope off to a tree, and then it was pretty easy to grab his hind legs and do the job."

The hog seemed less inclined to charge than previously. But he still remained watchful when we drew near, and he sometimes snapped his teeth together.

"He's taming down," Jack said, "and eating better. I believe he'll go three hundred pounds or more when he gets fat. He'll make a lot of meat."

On March 22, 1994, the *Wall Street Journal* featured a front-page article with the heading "Power Pork." It talked of a multibillion-dollar hog-production revolution taking shape, exemplified at a farm being built in Princeton, Missouri.

The *Journal*'s staff reporter, Scott Kilman, called the farm a factory. He described bulldozers leveling ground for metal barns that would house eighty thousand sows. The plan called for workers to install computers to monitor temperatures that, as in office buildings, would automatically adjust to fit the comfort ranges of the occupants. Sows would be artificially inseminated with sperm left by a boar in a dummy. Piglets, castrated at birth if they were males, would be taken from their mothers at eighteen days of age and raised in sterile, stainless steel cages. They would spend the remainder of their lives eating.

Hogs of market size, probably anticipating another day of eating, would instead leave their cages and slide down metal chutes into darkened rooms. Here, stunned by an electric prod, they would not feel it when their necks were slashed and their bodies hoisted by the hind legs to bleed. Computer-controlled machines would slice the bodies into uniformly packaged hams and chops, soon to be illuminated in refrigerated bins of grocery stores.

These megafarms have proved to be efficient at producing pork, wrote Kilman. The meat product has greater uniformity than that from family farms.

Kilman discussed the operation with a senior economist at the Federal Reserve Bank at Kansas City, the same bank that shortly after the Arab oil embargo twenty years earlier had worried about interruptions in the oil supply for fueling high-tech farms. No problem, said this economist: "We are on the cusp of a great change in agriculture."

One afternoon later that month as I drove into Plum Ridge, I noticed a man taking mail from his box near the street. He moved slowly. His stomach hid his belt in front, and his arms hung from the sleeves of his polo shirt like sausages. After shuffling through some envelopes, he moved back across the road and disappeared through the gate to his yard.

Later, at dusk, I noticed the same man standing at the other end of his yard where it overlooked the lake. He talked quietly with a companion. Often pausing for long periods to gaze across the water, he appeared to be searching for something. His head looked small on his massive body.

"He likes to eat," a neighbor had said. "Some people dig their graves with a spoon."

I recalled having seen this man on occasion driving into or out of Plum Ridge; he, like almost everyone in the little settlement, got his food in town. Once in a while he drove his golf cart down the street. Today at his mailbox was the first time I had seen him walk beyond the yard.

As the darkness thickened over the lake, he turned with his companion, and they slowly followed the chain link fence toward the lighted house fifty yards away. Waves spilled onto the sandy beach. The smell of grease sizzling on a grill came from somewhere. A metal gate clanked shut.

If a nation values anything more than freedom, it will lose its freedom; and . . . if it is comfort or money that it values more, it will lose that too.

W. Somerset Maugham, *Strictly Personal*

When asked about his ancestry, Corbett would say "Scotch-Irish" and that would end the interview. Not until I learned more about the history of those people did I associate Corbett's frugal nature with his ancestry.

For time unknown before Columbus, the Grahams had held a place among the people of the Scottish Highlands. Like other Highland clans, they wore a plaid design peculiar to the family name. They gained their sustenance from herding stock and from planting wheat. The modest quantities of beef and grain produced in that cool and foggy land kept the Highlanders lean and their numbers sparse.

Shortly following Columbus's landing in America, a different kind of crop made its way across the sea to Europe. It came from the high valleys and plateaus of the Andes Mountains. It proved supremely suited to the moist climate and organic soils of Scotland and Ireland.

Corbett grew this crop in his Peachtree garden but probably had no idea where it came from. He called it Irish potato.

Potatoes first showed up in Ireland in the early seventeenth century and within fifty years had become the staple food of the common people. It yielded much more food than traditional crops, fueling the fires of human reproduction. It boosted the population like a rocket.

Over generations, the Irish country people grew more and more dependent on this single crop. One observer noted that the sole food of Irish farmers often amounted to "potatoes and milk for ten months, and potatoes and salt the remaining two." The same observer estimated that each Irish man consumed a whopping twelve pounds of potatoes a day. Soon the dependence on potatoes spread to Scotland.

Some people worried about the burgeoning populations and their dependence on a single plant. Local potato crop failures prompted the Select Committee on the Advances for Public Works in Ireland to warn as early as 1835: "If the potato crop be a failure, its produce is consumed long before the peasantry can acquire new means of subsistence. . . ."

Disaster struck in summer 1845. Without warning and over wide areas, robustly growing potato plants shriveled, and, within days, nothing remained in the fields but black and withered stalks. A potato blight, caused by a kind of fungus infection, spread across the land. Fear clutched at the mothers of ten and eleven as they clawed at the ground, only to find the tubers as well beginning to rot. The next year the disease spread to the Scottish Highlands.

Over the next few years a million Irish and Scottish people starved to death. Travelers in the countryside saw the aftermath: "ten dead bodies out of eleven . . . in one cabin," "seven putrid corpses in another," and "dogs and swine quarrelling over, and fighting for, the dead carcasses of Christians." The subsidy had given out.

The greatest losses had fallen on the farmers who had depended almost exclusively on potatoes. Those remaining buried their dead, gathered up stray animals, and replanted their fields . . . to potatoes.

The 1994–1995 edition of the *Texas Almanac* shows that in 1850, when Texas had been open to Anglo settlement for thirty years and had been a state in the United States for five, only about two hundred thousand people lived within its borders. By the time Corbett's grand-father, Isaac, joined the army of immigrants into Texas just ten years later, the populace had tripled — to six hundred thousand. By Cor-bett's fifth year, it had hit the three million mark, and by 1950 it had passed seven million. Now there are seventeen million, with no end in sight. The same growth pattern prevails in Jasper County, the United States, and the world.

Such an unprecedented abundance of people came about because we learned to harness subsidies of energy from oil, gas, coal, and ura-nium. Applying corporate management and sophisticated technolo-gies to the acquisition and application of this energy, we rearranged materials and managed plants and animals to feed, clothe, and shelter ourselves. World War II and the industrial surge it generated kicked us into the final, ultimate technological orbit, and we flew higher than a people had ever flown before.

Corbett and Fannie cautiously tested the magic of this industrial journey. They bought automobiles and a tractor. They subscribed to REA and plugged in labor-saving gadgets. They even bought a televi-sion. But they kept one foot on the ground.

I likewise embraced the benefits of the industrial age. Machines may have seemed an indulgence to Corbett and Fannie, but to my brother, Jack, and me these were normal accoutrements of living, waiting to be claimed when we should reach the proper age. We got the blue bicycle when I turned eight.

Its previous owner had covered it with dull paint to hide the dings and rust, but we didn't object to its appearance. We wanted speed. After mastering the art of balancing, we got not only exhilarating speed but also a great leap in daily range down the gravel road that passed our house.

Frequent squabbles arose as to who would get to ride the bicycle. To gain the upper hand in one of these fights, I offered a deal to our mother, the arbitrator: let me ride the bike and I'll give you a fast ride down the hill. Clearly she must have seen through this ruse, but she finally agreed to the ride.

At the brink of the incline, I stood with one foot on the ground and the other poised on the opposite pedal. She climbed aboard behind me on the horizontal piece of perforated metal that served as a seat for passengers on all the old klunker bikes.

I pushed off, and we picked up speed. The wind whistled past. Then, as we reached the midpoint of the slope, I began to feel an unaccustomed wobble, caused I guess by the extra weight above the rear wheel. The bike began to fishtail, and then we hit a patch of gravel on the hard-packed clay. The world turned upside down.

We hit the ground and rolled. The bike skidded into the ditch. I escaped with minor scratches, but my mother lost big patches of skin from her arms, shoulders, and face. The machine had taught its first lesson.

By my early teens, my father decided Jack and I should learn to drive. He brought home a black Chevrolet car on its last legs, and we drove it far up into the pinewoods, where it broke down. Like Corbett the time his tractor had overturned, we were caught out on a limb. The anger of my father was worse than the forced walk home. He sold the car soon thereafter.

To replace the old car, my father bought my brother and me a small motorcycle. Its engine sounded like a lawn mower, and the exhaust pipe burned blisters when my bare legs brushed against it, but talk about mobility! Soon two of my friends had motorbikes of their own, and we explored the routes to neighboring towns. All of us somehow escaped serious injury, though one friend lost a lot of skin on a corner of the street in town.

The little Harley proved to be a fine way to get quickly into remote areas for squirrel hunting. Squeeze, the feist dog, would sit between my legs on the gas tank and weather the roughest rides. With a piece of string I would tie the rifle and any squirrels I bagged behind the seat.

I loved the convenience of cars and motorcycles, but they posed a problem. Other people had them, too, and there was nothing so awful as the sound of a stranger's motor in the woods. It signaled intrusion. A truck meant hunters or loggers. A motorboat on the river meant someone possibly headed for your fishing hole. The dreaded growl of an automobile creeping along a back road invariably sent me racing for a thicket or ravine to keep from being seen.

By graduation time at college, cheap cars and twenty-cents-a-gallon gasoline opened limitless horizons. I headed west, seeing Texas rapidly receding in the rearview mirror. I forgot about the bicycle accidents and automobile breakdowns. I had a newer car. Life in the Angelina country had begun to seem close and small.

Afterward, I stepped aboard an airplane. These machines shrank the distances even more, eventually taking me to far northern lands I had read about. I entered a countryside where people were accustomed to climbing far out on a limb by the sole support of airplanes. I climbed out with them.

We covered vast expanses that from the air looked uninhabited except for widely scattered villages. Once in a while we would see human figures standing tall above the tiny plants that cloaked the tundra, looking upward at our plane. Most had walked from somewhere else, I guess.

Were we intruding? I brushed the thought away.

Once we got stuck in a wilderness in Canada called Old Crow Flat. Five of us, including Billy Jacobson, an Eskimo, had flown into the area and landed on a lake. The floatplane left us there, promising to return the next day with food to replenish our supplies. It would have been impossible to walk out — frigid lakes and streams surrounded us in a vast and trackless land.

Two days passed, then three, then four. We ate what food was left. No plane arrived. Each day I listened with the others, intently, for a distant drone. But only loons broke the silence, and Billy Jacobson began to caress his rifle. He was waiting for the end of the fifth day, when the leader of our expedition had told him he could shoot the loons.

The time approached. We ate cranberries gathered from a local bog and watched the loons. The sun veered farther to the north. Then, just as Billy went inside the tent to get his rifle, I heard the sound, the blessed sound, of an airplane engine. Soon the swooping piece of steel lanced onto the lake, and its pontoons sent a rooster tail of spray into the air. Babbling with relief, we talked of steaks as the airplane cut its engines and drifted to the bank. From across the lake, the loons talked back.

It turned out that the pilot who had left us five days before had become marooned himself. En route to town, he had landed on a small lake to refuel from a gasoline cache. In taking off he had skidded his plane onto the bank, killing the propeller and radio. He escaped injury, but no one located him for three days.

Very soon after the plane arrived with food, the incident became a great adventure, not a problem. We forgot how hungry we had been.

The ordeal at Old Crow Flat seemed a minor inconvenience when I later saw how far out on a limb oil tempted others in that land. Barrow, Alaska, the same place where a white man's disease had killed off natives by the droves a hundred years before, received in the 1970s and 1980s a new infusion from the outside — royalties from oil discovered at Prudhoe Bay. With this they built new schools, new houses, and indoor swimming pools. All this in a climate where maintenance costs reached the sky.

They bought snow machines, airplanes, and motorboats. They switched from eating lots of fish and seal meat to beef steaks from the grocery store. Only the old folks talked about the old ways.

Prudhoe Bay will be pumped dry in twenty years, I heard the oilmen say in the latter 1980s. What then, I wondered. Corbett might have had something to say about it had he known.

After Fannie died, Corbett grew listless at the Peachtree farm. The cows mostly fed themselves, the TV and radio had little relevant to say, and the dishes that he used could be daily washed in fifteen minutes. He tinkered with the tractor and hoed weeds in the garden.

Jack and I had taken off to other interests and places. The neighbors seldom visited. Boose and Versie down the road needed little help; they were self-sufficient. Corbett's brothers and his sister had their own lives, too, and lived away.

One day he pumped up the tires on the old '49 Ford pickup parked beneath the corncrib roof. He took a piece of haywire and twisted it with pliers onto the valve-stem of one tire to stop the leaking. He pressed the starter, and the engine cranked right up.

Later, a man came with a flat-bottomed aluminum boat, a 6-horsepower motor, and a boat trailer. He left with the pickup.

It had been a year since Fannie died when I brought my wife and six-month-old son to visit. Corbett didn't know what to do with the baby; he held him motionless on his knee, and his lower jaw quivered. Maybe he wished Fannie could have seen him.

He offered to take my wife and me fishing. We talked about where to go.

"Those piney-woods creeks where we used to take you boys to catch bream are all closed up now," he said. "Posted. We could go up to Rayburn Lake, but those people get in a hurry, and they could swamp my little boat.

"Let's go down to the Forks of the river," he finally decided.

The Forks. I recalled it as it had been ten years before, a quiet criss-crossing of sloughs between the Angelina and Neches Rivers just above their juncture.

"I don't think many people go in there, even now," he said.

Versie and Boose said they would watch the baby. Corbett hooked the boat trailer to his '60 Ford car, and we drove to the Bevilport landing on the Angelina. The river flowed dark and clear. New houses watched from nearby; they had sprung up since the completion of the dam upstream.

"Don't forget the paddle," he said as we climbed into the boat.

We motored downstream. We met other boats, mostly bigger than ours and faster. Corbett would slow the motor each time one passed, nosing his boat into the wake to keep from shipping water.

Finally, we slowed and veered toward the riverbank. He brushed aside a leaning willow branch, pushed at a raft of driftwood with the paddle, and slid the boat into a stump-filled slough.

Thirty minutes down the amber waterway, he tied the boat off to a cypress stump, and we baited up the crappie hooks. He didn't have much to say.

I listened. The sound of motorboats had died. The "killy-killy" of a red-shouldered hawk echoed from the nearby woods; something slapped the water just around the bend.

Suddenly Corbett's bobber went under, and he snapped the tip of his cane pole into the air. He fought a crappie to the surface and pulled it into the boat.

"Catch it before it sinks!" he called as the fish thumped against the aluminum bottom. His jaw was shaking.

"It" turned out to be his bait, a now-broken minnow. I leaned over the edge of the boat and got it just before it disappeared from sight. Corbett gave a chuckle and threaded it back onto his hook.

The fish kept biting, and the sun sank behind the trees before we left the Forks that day. The other boats had abandoned the darkening water by the time we pulled up to the ramp at Bevilport. A barred owl's "hoo-hoo-hooahh!" came rolling down the river. It had been a good day.

*"Let's go down to the Forks." A cypress and palmetto slough where the Angelina
meets the Neches—a fine place to travel back in time.*

"Three fish with one bait," Corbett said for at least the third time.
Something had happened inside, and he talked. In the dusk his face
looked peaceful, satisfied.

By the spring of 1967, approaching two years after Fannie's
death, Corbett seemed to have regained more of his old spirit. He

helped with the upkeep of the Peachtree pasture in springtime and in summer. It needed mowing to keep out invading shrubs and trees, and at these times he kept the bush-hog hooked to his beloved tractor. Because the mower weighed several hundred pounds and had a thick steel blade, it could clear the toughest brush. It could be raised or lowered by the tractor's hydraulic lift.

When mowing, you had to watch for humps and potholes, especially where the windrows of the bulldozed trees once had been burned. Remnants of stumps and mounds of clay that had been thrown up with roots remained here and there.

One morning near mid-May, Corbett decided to mow the pasture behind Boose and Versie's fence. He drove the tractor down and started mowing four-foot swaths, back and forth. By mid-morning he had edged into a strip of land where lumpy ground told him to be careful.

He raised the bush-hog off the ground and started into a turn when the tractor turned against him. The outer rear wheel hit a clay-root hidden in the weeds. The governor to the engine's gas supply poured on extra power, as it always did when the tractor got into a strain. The sudden burst of forward motion against the clay-packed hump snapped the wheel high into the air. The weight of the bush-hog added extra momentum, and the tractor flipped completely over.

Later that morning Boose went outside and saw smoke rising from the pasture. He moved to get a better look and saw the rear wheels of the tractor in the air. Racing down, he saw a fire eating at the grass. Corbett lay lifeless, pinned face-down beneath the bush-hog, his shoe and overalls burned off one leg.

22 **Hope**

For to him that is joined to all the living there is hope. . . .
Ecclesiastes 9 : 4

When Prometheus gave heaven's fire to mortals, it made the Greek gods angry. They created a beautiful woman, Pandora, and sent her to earth with a closed box full of mischief, knowing her curiosity would eventually make her open it. Sure enough, after some years she peeked inside the box. War, Pestilence, and Hunger escaped, spreading around the world. She quickly slammed the lid, but too late. The damage had been done.

Only one thing remained inside: Hope.

My geography teacher in grade school told us that the primary necessities of human life were food and shelter. My Sunday school instructor talked about the importance of hope. Corbett taught me that all three came from land and that the greatest of them was hope.

"I hope we catch some fish today," he would say on our way to the Angelina River or to one of the pinewoods streams that fed it.

My heart would race, and I would imagine a great fish plunging to the depths of a dark pool with my hook in its mouth. I would squirm anxiously on the seat of the '49 Ford pickup, squeezed in by Corbett, Fannie, and the black-knobbed floor shift. The pickup seemed painfully slow. It bounced over tree roots that erosion had exposed in the narrow road and sloshed through mudholes as it strained to reach the fishing hole.

Then I left the Angelina country. My years in school accumulated, and soon everybody said my knowledge far surpassed Corbett's. I took a job in town, and the check I got each month would have taken him a year to earn, sharpening saws.

But something seemed amiss. Food had lost the flavor I remembered, and the rooms I inhabited looked out on treeless streets and smelled like carpet cleaner. The money coming in, which at first had generated anticipation, became expected, certain. Hope diminished.

The head man of our company came around one day and said, look, we're going to give you part of the company. Here's a certificate for a thousand shares of stock. I felt better and went back to work with renewed vigor.

The company grew, and so did my pay. The head man called us all together and told about even greater opportunities in store. The bank had loaned the company more money, he said, and we had invested in a great new opportunity.

But the sure thing failed. The head man called us together again. He poured himself a gin and tonic. Look, we're going bankrupt. We have to restructure.

The stock certificates? Oh, well, they have no value now. You understand.

Later on, I read about a story by Franz Kafka, the novelist, about a kind of hopelessness he called passive hope. A man comes to the door to heaven and asks admittance. He is told to wait, which he does, for days, then years. He repeatedly asks to enter, but the doorkeeper repeatedly says not yet. Finally, old and near death, the man finds the door suddenly shut in his face by the gatekeeper.

The bureaucrats had the last word. The old man's entry did not fit their agenda. If the man had had the courage in his youth to disregard them, this act would have liberated him to pursue his own route to the shining palace. Instead, he waited on the word of the gatekeeper.

I began to think about what had generated hope back in the Angelina country. Food comes from land, not grocery stores, Corbett had showed me. Feeding too habitually at the company table bears the risk of trading freedom for the promise of security and losing hope, I decided.

I remembered the uncommon skill and pleasure Corbett and Fannie showed in getting food from the land about them. Each fresh hog track and each new seedling bursting from the soil kindled hope.

Here's how you find a bee tree. We'll put honey out on this stump, come back after noon, and maybe find some bees on it. When one leaves, it may circle, but then it will head out on a line.

Look, there goes one now! There's another one going in the same direction. Probably there's a tub of honey if we can find the tree. Let's go; it can't be far away!

In those days I found myself forever trying to peek backward in time. Windows to the past had a special quality — they not only glorified the present, they sometimes let me speculate about the future. They were excellent for generating hope.

I remember where the rocks narrowed the river channel at the mouth of Mill Creek. Corbett said the Indians used to set fish traps there when the river got its lowest during summer. Halfway through a summer's day, picking peas, I would drift off in my mind to that flat rock and ease my hook into the channel.

Once, while wading in the shallows of Sam Rayburn Lake just out from Plum Ridge, my mother saw a thin triangle on the sandy bottom. She plunged her arm beneath the surface, bringing up a spearpoint longer than her hand. It dwarfed an ordinary arrowhead. A flint of mottled gray and brown, it clearly had been built by a master's hand an unknown space of years before.

"It came from someplace else," said one of Boose's friends who claimed to know about such things. "That kind of flint can't be found in these parts."

When I touched the stone, I could feel the magic, the hope, of another time.

What was it about the spoor of ancient people on the land that had kindled hope in me when I was young, when sign of modern ones later caused such hopelessness? Perhaps the ancients spoke of simpler times, of other possibilities, while contemporary people threatened with their noise, their numbers, and their closing off of options. It began to seem to me that time more easily accommodated people than did space.

Living in a city cubicle for years, I learned a spectator's relationship with land. I ate food from fields but never felt the hope at planting. I sent my waste away in trucks and pipes to a place guaranteed to be sanitary. On the television screen I saw places where hope's dimension had been lost.

Corbett and Fannie had lived with land as provider, adversary, companion. Can you eat it? Will it bite you? Can you catch a fish in it or find a shelter from the rain? The best figs grow beside the outdoor toilet. They participated, and perhaps because of this, they hoped. Maybe I didn't know as much as they did after all.

Corbett and Fannie have been gone almost thirty years. The oaks and maples I planted in a corner of that cornfield Corbett used to plow have grown and now bear seeds. The soil there has softened and turned darker. Deer and coyote tracks make dents in gopher mounds among the dewberry vines.

I don't live there anymore, but I have put one foot back on the land. Hope has rediscovered me. It was always around, really, it's just that I had strayed too far away from the exciting uncertainty offered by land and too far toward the deadening security promised on paper.

Now when I turn the soil in spring and plant the corn and bean seeds saved from last year, I hope they will sprout. Maybe this year there will be a bumper crop. Though I never can be 100 percent sure exactly what will happen in the short term — it may come a drought — the years have taught me that if I listen to the land and treat it right, it will in the long run do the same for me.

Corbett's there, and Fannie, too, hoping with me. Life has come full circle. I know they're glad that I did not forget the paddle.

Bibliography

Anyou, R., and S. A. LeBlanc. 1984. *The Galaz ruin: A prehistoric Mimbres village in southwestern New Mexico*. Albuquerque: Maxwell Museum of Anthropology and University of New Mexico Press.

Baxter, Gordon. 1991. It really is Mr. Sam's lake. In *Catch the best, Jasper, Texas*. Jasper: Jasper Chamber of Commerce.

Bennett, H., and P. Marcus. 1951. *Ford: We never called him Henry*. New York: Tom Doherty Associates.

Block, W. T. n.d. Mill towns and ghost towns of East Texas: Some early sawmills, shingle mills, tram roads, and logging camps of Jasper County, Texas. N.p.

Bolton, Herbert E., ed. 1908. *Spanish exploration in the Southwest, 1542–1706*. New York: Barnes and Noble Books.

Bowman, Robert. 1990. *The 35 best ghost towns in East Texas*. Lufkin, Tex.: Best of East Texas Publishers.

Brower, Charles D. 1942. *Fifty years below zero: A lifetime of adventure in the far North*. New York: Dodd, Mead.

Caro, R. A. 1990. *The years of Lyndon Johnson: Means of ascent*. New York: Alfred A. Knopf.

Chandler, L. V. 1970. *America's greatest depression, 1929–1941*. New York: Harper & Row.

Chapman, J., H. R. Delcourt, and P. A. Delcourt. 1989. Strawberry fields, almost forever. *Natural History* (Sept. 1989): 51–58.

Cole, E. W. 1946. La Salle in Texas. *Southwestern Historical Quarterly* 49: 473–500.

Comeaux, M. L. 1972. *Atchafalaya swamp life: Settlement and folk occupations*. Baton Rouge: Louisiana State University School of Geoscience.

Corkran, D. H. 1967. *The Creek frontier, 1540–1783*. Norman: University of Oklahoma Press.

Cronon, W., and R. White. 1986. Indians in the land. *American Heritage* 37: 18–25.

Cruikshank, J. W., and I. F. Eldredge. 1939. *Forest resources of southeastern Texas*. Washington, D.C.: U.S. Department of Agriculture Miscellaneous Publications No. 326.

Dary, David. 1981. *Cowboy culture: A saga of five centuries*. New York: Avon Books.

Delcourt, P. A. 1980. Goshen Springs: Late Quaternary vegetation record for southern Alabama. *Ecology* 61: 371–386.

Diemer, H. 1909. *Automobiles*. Chicago: American School of Correspondence.

Dobie, J. F. 1939. The first cattle in Texas and the Southwest progenitors of the longhorn. *Southwestern Historical Quarterly* 42: 171–197.

Duffy, J. W. 1964. *Power, prime mover of technology*. Bloomington, Ill.: McKnight & McKnight.

Fagan, Brian, M. 1987. *The great journey: The peopling of ancient America*. New York: Thames and Hudson.

———. 1990. *The journey from Eden: The peopling of our world*. New York: Thames and Hudson.

———. 1991. *Kingdoms of gold, kingdoms of jade: The Americas before Columbus*. New York: Thames and Hudson.

Foreman, G. 1934. *The five civilized tribes: Cherokee, Chickasaw, Choctaw, Creek, Seminole*. Norman: University of Oklahoma Press.

Galbraith, J. K. 1967. *The new industrial state*. Boston: Houghton Mifflin.

Gant, J. H. 1905. Original field notes on mammals and birds of Hardin County, Texas. Washington, D.C.: Smithsonian Institution Archives.

Gomery, D. 1993. As the dial turns. *Wilson Quarterly* 42: 41–46.

Haynes, G. 1991. *Mammoths, mastodons, and elephants: Biology, behavior, and the fossil record*. New York: Cambridge University Press.

Hinkelbein, Albert. 1971. *Energy and power*. New York: Franklin Watts.

House, B. 1941. *Oil boom: The story of Spindletop, Burk-burnett, Mexia, Smackover, Desdemona, and Ranger*. Caldwell, Ind.: Catton Printers.

Huxley, Aldous. 1932. *Brave new world*. New York: Harper and Brothers.

Jordan, T. G. 1981. *Trails to Texas: Southern roots of western cattle ranching*. Lincoln: University of Nebraska Press.

Kilman, Scott. 1994. Power pork: Corporations begin to turn hog business into an assembly line. *Wall Street Journal*, March 22, 1994.

Kingston, M., and M. G. Crawford, eds. 1993. *Texas Almanac, 1994–95*. Dallas: *Dallas Morning News*.

Kunitz, S. J., and R. C. Euler. 1972. Aspects of southwestern paleoepidemiology. *Prescott College Anthropological Report*, No. 2. (Prescott, Ariz.).

Lacey, R. 1986. *Ford: The men and the machine*. Boston: Little, Brown.

Lasswell, Mary. 1967. John Henry Kirby: Prince of the pines. N.p.

Lay, D. W. 1938. Opossum status studied. *Texas Game, Fish, and Oyster Commission Monthly Bulletin*, No. 1.

———. 1939. Fur resources of eastern Texas. *Texas Game, Fish, and Oyster Commission Monthly Bulletin*, No. 15.

McWilliams, R. G. 1953. *Fleur de Lys and Calumet: Being the Penicaut narrative of French adventure in Louisiana.* Tuscaloosa: University of Alabama Press.

Martin, Paul S. 1984. Prehistoric overkill: The global model. In P. S. Martin and R. G. Klein, eds., *Quaternary extinctions.* Tucson: University of Arizona Press.

Maxwell, R. S., and R. D. Baker. 1983. *Sawdust empire: The Texas lumber industry, 1830–1940.* College Station: Texas A & M University Press.

Miller, G. Tyler. 1991. *Environmental science: Sustaining the earth.* Belmont, Calif.: Wadsworth.

Morfi, J. A. 1935. *History of Texas, 1673–1779.* Translated by C. E. Castaneda. Albuquerque: Quivira Society.

Newell, J. A. 1934. Early cattle raising in East Texas. *Cattleman* (February 1934).

Nye, D. E. 1979. *Henry Ford: "Ignorant idealist."* Port Washington, N.Y.: Kennikat Press.

Oberholser, H. C. 1902. Original field notes on mammals and birds in the vicinity of Jasper, Texas. Washington, D.C.: Smithsonian Institution Archives.

Owen-Smith, Norman. 1987. Pleistocene extinctions: The pivotal role of megaherbivores. *Paleobiology* 13: 351–362.

———. 1989. Megafaunal extinctions: The conservation message from 11,000 years B.P. *Conservation Biology* 3: 405–412.

Owsley, Frank L. 1949. *Plain folk of the Old South.* Chicago: Quadrangle Books.

Packard, V. 1957. *The hidden persuaders.* New York: David McKay.

Parkman, Francis. 1879. *La Salle and the discovery of the great West.* New York: New American Library of World Literature.

Perrigo, Lynn I. 1960. *Texas and our Spanish Southwest.* Dallas: Banks Upshaw.

Peterson, H. L., and R. Elman. 1971. *The great guns.* New York: Grosset & Dunlap and the Ridge Press.

Redford, Kent H. 1992. The empty forest. *BioScience* 42: 412–422.

Rostlund, Erhard. 1960. The geographic range of the historic bison in the Southeast. *Annals of the Association of American Geographers* 50: 395–407.

Salaman, R. N. 1949. *The history and social influence of the potato.* London: Cambridge University Press.

Severy, M. 1992. Portugal's sea road to the East. *National Geographic* 182: 56–93.

Snow, Dean R. 1989. *The archaeology of North America.* New York: Chelsea House.

Steinberg, A. 1975. *Sam Rayburn: A biography.* New York: Hawthorn Books.

Swanton, J. R. 1942. *Source material on the history and ethnology of the Caddo Indians.* Washington, D.C.: Smithsonian Institution, Bureau of American Ethnology, Bulletin 132.

Taylor, J. 1955. *Pondoro: Last of the ivory hunters*. New York: Simon and Schuster.

Texas Game, Fish, and Oyster Commission. 1929. *Review of Texas wild life and conservation*. Austin.

Turnbull, Colin M. 1961. The forest people: A study of the Pygmies of the Congo. New York: Simon and Schuster.

U.S. Army Corps of Engineers. 1987. *Sam Rayburn Dam and Reservoir*.

U.S. Forest Service. 1988. *The South's fourth forest: Alternatives for the future*. Washington, D.C.: U.S. Department of Agriculture Forest Resource Report No. 24.

Van Doren, M., ed. 1928. *Travels of William Bartram*. New York: Dover.

Webb, W. P., and H. B. Carroll, eds. 1952. *The handbook of Texas*. Austin: Texas State Historical Association.

White, R. 1983. *The roots of dependency: Subsistence, environment, and social change among the Choctaws, Pawnees, and Navajos*. Lincoln: University of Nebraska Press.

Williams, Paul R. 1985. Excavations at Oak Creek Valley Pueblo. Master's thesis, Northern Arizona University.

Williams, R. C. 1987. *Fordson, Farmall, and Poppin' Johnny: A history of the farm tractor and its impact on America*. Urbana: University of Illinois Press.

Wills, W. H. 1989. Patterns of prehistoric food production in west-central New Mexico. *Journal of Anthropological Research* 45: 139–157.

Wright, S. A. 1942. *My rambles as East Texas cowboy, hunter, fisherman, tie-cutter*. Austin: Texas Folklore Society.

Wyman, Walker D. 1945. *The wild horse of the West*. Lincoln: University of Nebraska Press.

Youngquist, W. 1990. *Mineral resources and the destinies of nations*. Portland, Ore.: National Book Company.